Close Reading the Media

Teach middle school students to become savvy consumers of the TV, print, and online media bombarding them every day. In this timely book copublished by Routledge and MiddleWeb, media literacy expert Frank W. Baker offers thematic lessons for every month of the school year, so you can engage students in learning by having them analyze the real world around them. Students will learn to think critically about photos, advertisements, and other media and consider the intended purposes and messages. Topics include:

- helping students detect fake news;
- unraveling the messages in TV advertising;
- looking at truth vs propaganda in political ads and debates;
- revealing how big media influences the news we read;
- understanding how pictures changed America during the Civil Rights Movement;
- exploring the language of film and the symbols of costume design;
- thinking about how media appeals to our emotions;
- examining branding, product placement, and the role of celebrity;
- reading and interpreting iconic news images;
- and much, much more!

In addition, the book's lesson plans contain connections to key standards and step-by-step activities you can use immediately. With this practical book, you'll have all the tools and ideas you need to help today's students successfully navigate their media-filled world.

Frank W. Baker is a renowned media literacy expert who holds workshops for teachers across the country. He is an educational consultant to the Writing Improvement Network and the News Literacy Project, as well as a blogger for MiddleWeb. He is also the author of *Media Literacy in the K-12 Classroom* (ISTE, 2016) and co-author of *Mastering Media Literacy* with Heidi Hayes Jacobs (Solution Tree, 2013). Visit his website, frankwbaker.com.

I0892465

Also Available from Routledge Eye On Education and MiddleWeb
(www.routledge.com/collections/11190)

Write, Think, Learn: Tapping the Power of Daily Student Writing Across the Content Areas
Mary K. Tedrow

Creating Citizens: Teaching Civics and Current Events in the History Classroom, 6–9
Sarah Cooper

The Genius Hour Guidebook: Fostering Passion, Wonder, and Inquiry in the Classroom
Denise Krebs and Gallit Zvi

STEM by Design: Strategies and Activities for Grades 4–8
Anne Jolly

The Flexible ELA Classroom: Practical Tools for Differentiated Instruction in Grades 4–8
Amber Chandler

History Class Revisited: Tools and Projects to Engage Middle School Students in Social Studies
Jody Passanisi

Two Teachers in the Room: Strategies for Co-Teaching Success
Elizabeth Stein

Close Reading the Media

Literacy Lessons and Activities for Every Month of the School Year

Frank W. Baker

Routledge
Taylor & Francis Group
NEW YORK AND LONDON

MiddleWeb
All About the Middle Grades

First published 2018
by Routledge
711 Third Avenue, New York, NY 10017

and by Routledge
2 Park Square, Milton Park, Abingdon, Oxon, OX14 4RN

Routledge is an imprint of the Taylor & Francis Group, an informa business

Library of Congress Cataloging-in-Publication Data
A catalog record for this book has been requested

ISBN: 978-1-138-21600-6 (hbk)
ISBN: 978-1-138-21602-0 (pbk)
ISBN: 978-1-315-44304-1 (ebk)

Typeset in Palatino
by Swales & Willis Ltd, Exeter, Devon, UK

Contents

Meet the Author

Frank W. Baker began his career as a TV weatherman. He worked for nine years in television news, mostly as a newscast producer. He left TV news to join the Orange County Public School System (Orlando, FL) where he oversaw distance education and instructional TV for 11 years. In 1999, his seminal study of how media literacy was represented in state teaching standards was a significant step in helping educators recognize the importance of media literacy education.

Baker's popular Media Literacy Clearinghouse website (www.frankwbaker.com/mlc) is a frequently updated resource created for educators. He is the author of three books: *Coming Distractions: Questioning Movies* (Capstone Press); *Political Campaigns & Political Advertising: A Media Literacy Guide* (ABC-CLIO); and *Media Literacy in the K-12 Classroom*, 2nd Edition (ISTE). He has contributed chapters to *Mastering Media Literacy* (Solution Tree Press); *The Prager Handbook of Media Literacy* (ABC-CLIO); *Curriculum 21* (ASCD); *Lesson Plans for Creating Media Rich Classrooms* (NCTE); and *Visions/Revisions: Moving Forward With Media Education* (National Telemedia Council).

In South Carolina, where he resides, Baker helped write the state's English and Visual/Performing Arts Teaching standards, which include media literacy. He has conducted hundreds of workshops for teachers in the United States and abroad in support of integrating media literacy across the curriculum.

Baker was honored in 2013 with the Jessie McCanse Award, given by the National Telemedia Council for lifetime contributions to the field of media literacy. In 2015, he edited a special issue of NTC's *Journal of Media Literacy* which examined media literacy through the lens of Common Core State Standards.

In 2012, Baker became a regular contributor of media literacy articles at MiddleWeb.com, where founder and co-editor John Norton described Baker as "the most media-literate educator in America." In 2017, MiddleWeb launched a monthly column by Baker titled "Close Reading the Media."

Frank wants to dedicate this book to his wife Melanie, his kids Bryan, Paige, and Josh, and his granddaughter Sadie.

Introduction

It's the start of another one of my "media literacy" workshops for teachers. I begin, as always, with the question: What is media literacy? I ask participants to turn off their computers or tablets and simply write, in their own words, what they think that phrase means.

The answers are wide ranging and sometimes surprising. And, as always, consensus on a definition is elusive.

Yet we can agree that we live in a media-saturated world. Everywhere we turn it seems someone is out to sell you something or to persuade you in some way. But we are so immersed that it's not always easy to discern what's going on.

Many educators have told me that their students don't question media: they believe most everything they see, read, or hear. There is way too much media illiteracy out there at a time when having the skills and knowledge to deconstruct the media onslaught is becoming an urgent priority.

When I began the Media Literacy Clearinghouse website (www.frankwbaker.com), I created a sort-of slogan: *Critical thinking about media messages.* Pretty simple.

I define media literacy as applying critical thinking skills to all that we experience in the media. But media literacy is much more than just critical thinking. It implies an understanding of the economics behind the messaging and an appreciation of the techniques used by media-makers as they take aim at our heads and hearts.

Being "media literate" implies that we can control the media rather than have it control us. In the classroom, media literacy is about "close reading" what we hear and see – asking students to not only analyze media messages but to learn more deeply by creating messages themselves.

Media Literacy Is a Subject Worthy of Deep Study

In 1999, I conducted a content analysis of the teaching standards in all 50 states. I was hoping to find evidence of media literacy expectations and I did. Almost every state had some elements of media literacy in the teaching standards for English/Language Arts, Health, or Social Studies. That was good news, and that trend has continued and strengthened in the early 21st century with the rise of the internet and 24/7 media access.

The bad news, then and now, is that despite these stated expectations, media literacy is not often taught in our K-12 classrooms. It's not tested and few textbooks address it in any sustained and meaningful way, although many are starting to include some elements of media literacy as "sidebar material."

In "Why Core Standards Must Embrace Media Literacy," an op-ed I co-authored for Education Week in 2011, my colleague Richard Beach and I complained about the lack of media literacy representation in the Common Core English language arts (ELA) standards (www.edweek.org/ew/articles/2011/06/22/36baker.h30.html). We wrote:

> there is no specific reference in the common standards to critical analysis and production of film, television, advertising, radio, news, music, popular culture, video games, media remixes, and so on. Nor is there explicit attention on fostering critical analysis of media messages and representations.

Despite its shortcomings, there are places in the Common Core State Standards where media literacy is implied, most specifically when they cite the general need to "evaluate information from multiple oral, visual, or multimodal sources." (See Chapter 4, Lesson 11, for more on this.)

While the Common Core doesn't exactly embrace media literacy, two major educational organizations have. The National Council of Teachers of English (NCTE) has recommended consistently over the years that educators include "non-print texts" in their lessons. Most ELA teachers know that "informational texts" include film, television, magazines, newspapers, and advertising – exactly the types of media I believe we must engage students in analyzing critically. Here is what NCTE said in its resolution on "promoting media literacy," first published in 1975:

> This resolution grew out of awareness among educators that understanding the new media and using them constructively and creatively actually required developing a new form of literacy – new critical abilities "in reading, listening, viewing, and thinking" that would enable students to deal constructively with complex new modes of delivering information, new multisensory tactics for persuasion, and new technology-based art forms.
>
> (www.ncte.org/positions/statements/promotingmedialit)

Social studies educators are also familiar with addressing the impact of media in history and civics lessons. Most state standards reference:

- the rise of mass media in history;
- the role of propaganda;
- primary sources (including photos and printed images);
- the role of media in the election process;
- advertising as a part of economics.

In spring 2016, the National Council for the Social Studies (NCSS) published a revision to its Position Statement on Media Literacy. The new statement, which I helped co-author, says:

> Through the decoding of content-rich media texts in the social studies classroom, students learn and practice the habits of asking key questions, applying historical analysis, identifying perspective, assessing credibility, providing text-based evidence, drawing conclusions, and reflecting on their own process of reasoning.
>
> (www.socialstudies.org/publications/socialeducation/may-june2016/media-literacy)

The statement goes on to provide educators with more justification for engaging students in thoughtful inquiry, analysis, and deconstruction, understanding media language and propaganda techniques, understanding media economics, and much more.

Media Literacy Requires Critical Inquiry

One of the major goals of media literacy is to promote critical inquiry – asking questions.

Critical inquiry is also a large part of the new College, Career & Civic Life C3 Framework for Social Studies State Standards (www.socialstudies.org/system/files/c3/C3-Framework-for-Social-Studies.pdf). The C3 Framework encompasses four dimensions, each of which is a good fit with the objectives of media literacy (see Table I.1).

For many readers of this book, the C3 may feel brand new . . . I hope social studies educators in your area are planning professional development around these dimensions as they search for ways to better engage the 21st-century learner.

Table I.1 The College, Career & Civic Life C3 Framework for Social Studies State Standards

<table>
<tr><td>Dimension 1: Developing questions and planning inquiries</td><td>Dimension 2: Applying disciplinary tools and concepts</td><td>Dimension 3: Evaluating sources and using evidence</td><td>Dimension 4: Communicating conclusions and taking informed action</td></tr>
<tr><td rowspan="4">Developing questions and planning inquiries</td><td>Civics</td><td rowspan="2">Gathering and evaluating sources</td><td rowspan="2">Communicating and critiquing conclusions</td></tr>
<tr><td>Economics</td></tr>
<tr><td>Geography</td><td rowspan="2">Developing claims and using evidence</td><td rowspan="2">Taking informed action</td></tr>
<tr><td>History</td></tr>
</table>

Media Literacy Learning Throughout the School Year

In 2012, I approached the editors at MiddleWeb.com to express an interest in submitting an essay that explored ways middle-grades educators might connect popular culture and current events to media literacy. The article found an audience and led to a continuing series of guest articles on media literacy topics – numbering more than three dozen at this writing. Our publishing partnership also became the genesis of this book.

What follows are my suggestions for how to engage students in media literacy throughout the school year. I've included ideas that I have field-tested with teachers during more than 20 years of work in classrooms and as part of professional development workshops.

This text aims to provide month-by-month ideas, recommendations, and resources for incorporating media literacy into instruction. It draws on my MiddleWeb articles where I examined popular culture and timely news events and offered them as opportunities to engage your students in critical inquiry and media study. I've also included new and supplemental material to create what I hope is a unique resource for the ELA or social studies classroom.

My goal is to help you feel more comfortable teaching media literacy with your students. The first chapter offers some background on media literacy. Subsequent chapters cover topics as diverse as news, magazines, movies, television, advertising, and more. Be sure to check out the recommended resources listed throughout each chapter. And feel free to rearrange lessons as you see fit to meet your curriculum needs. The seasonal suggestions are just that – suggestions.

It is my hope – no, my desire – that you will find the topics both relevant and engaging for your students as you prepare them to be effective media communicators and creative producers in the 21st century. These skills have never been more relevant to adult success or more important to sustaining a civil society.

I maintain a Facebook page (www.facebook.com/medialiteracyman) and a Twitter account (@fbaker) where I post daily about media, media issues, and media literacy. Please follow me there and at my MiddleWeb column "Close Reading the Media" – and be sure to share your own insights and examples of the work you and your students are doing.

Frank W. Baker

Website with Accompanying Media

As this is a book on media literacy, we naturally want to show you more media images and videos than would be possible to include in a print book. Therefore, as you read, you'll see a box called Media Link, marked with this icon 🌐. This means there is a full-color photograph or video to accompany the lesson, available on Frank Baker's website so you can display it and analyze it with students. Each Media Link box includes the URL for that lesson's image.

August

This opening chapter will introduce you and your students to media literacy and the art of asking questions. Among other things, media literacy seeks to raise your students' awareness of how much time they spend with media, because frankly they don't know. This chapter and its resources are designed to provide a framework for the remaining chapters, so you might wish to conduct these activities first before moving on.

The Common Core teaching standards emphasize "close reading," so you'll find an abundance of ideas and resources for engaging your students at deeper levels of comprehension.

LESSON 1

Exploring Media Literacy with Students

Background

Teachers can use this "defining" exercise to introduce the media literacy "big idea" to students and explore some facets of media literacy education.

Look up any published definition of media literacy and you're likely to find *analyze* and *create* (or its less robust synonym *produce*) – two words associated with higher-order thinking skills. Most teachers would expect to have students "analyze" media as part of literacy learning. Media literacy educators believe it is also important to have them "create" media as a way to gain a deeper understanding of how persuasion and the manipulation of words and images can be used to shape our thoughts and desires. You'll want to make sure you introduce both these concepts as you work through this activity.

Here are two often-cited definitions of media literacy to keep in mind. You may wish to present these to students during or after the exercise described below.

This succinct definition was crafted by a conference of educators in 1992:

> A media-literate person . . . can access, analyze, evaluate, and produce both print and electronic media.
>
> (www.medialit.org/reading-room/aspen-media-literacy-conference-report-part-ii)

This longer, richer definition (one of my favorites) was written by the Ontario Ministry of Education in 1989:

> Media Literacy is concerned with helping students develop an informed and critical understanding of the nature of mass media, the techniques used by them and the impact of these techniques. More specifically, it is education that aims to increase students' understanding and enjoyment of how the media work, how they produce meaning, how they are organized, and how they construct reality. Media literacy also aims to provide students with the ability to create media products.
>
> (www.medialit.org/reading-room/what-media-literacy-canadian-definition)

Activity: Defining Media Literacy

1. In your classroom (on the board or some other visible place) create two columns with the words MEDIA and LITERACY where you can make a list under each term.
2. Ask your students to imagine they're going on a train ride across the USA and they can use only one medium to keep up with what's going on. What would it be? Their answers will be written under the column you've created that says MEDIA. Many are likely to immediately say "a smartphone." List this and any other choices. Then share a simple definition of the word. *MEDIA: A means of mass communication.* Ask students if the items on the list meet this definition. Strike any that do not.
3. Ask what other things might meet the definition. Do they mention books, magazines, television programs, radio, billboards, the Internet, movies, theater, social media apps, music? Add any missing media to the growing list. Depending on the size of your group, choose some or all of the mediums on the list and divide into subgroups.
4. Assign each group one form of media (you might have the forms of media printed on index cards, so you'd be distributing one card to each group). In their groups, they'll have 10 minutes to come up with answers to these questions:

    1. Three good things about my medium are . . .
    2. Three not-so-good things are . . .
    3. On a scale from 1–10, how good would my medium be at mass communication? Why?
    4. Would advertisers want to use my medium? Why or why not?

5. At the end of the 10 minutes, a representative of each group shares their responses.
6. Next, ask your students to define the word LITERACY. Note some responses in the column. If most of the focus is on reading and writing skills, share the second definition of *LITERACY: Competence or knowledge in a specified area.* Then ask, "What else might we need to be literate about? Do the examples of media we've identified give us any clues?" Add other literacy examples to the list. Then teachers might ask "Which of these literacies might have special importance in today's digital world?" If it hasn't come up, students might be encouraged to think about visual literacy – the ability to comprehend the messages behind all the images we see today in mass media. The teacher might model a few examples of "reading an image."

7. Then ask your students: "How many of you have ever created some form of media?" Their responses can include anything from artwork to music, a video, a poem, even a movie. Students love to be able to make media. With cameras now a part of every mobile phone, computer, and e-tablet, they are already broadcasters and movie makers. Ask, "If you've created a form of media, what messages did you communicate? Was it effective? Why?"
8. Now have students write a 1–2-sentence definition of "media literacy."

Teaching tip: When I've asked my audiences (groups of educators) to define media literacy, many of them understand the importance of analyzing or questioning media messages, but many of them do not include the fact that media literacy is also about giving students opportunities to create media with conscious attention to the messages they want to communicate.

Simply put, ANALYSIS + PRODUCTION = MEDIA LITERACY

This activity helps put media literacy into perspective. By first having students think critically about media and what media literacy means, we help them appreciate the fact that the various mediums are powerful and work on us in different ways. I am a strong advocate for teaching media literacy skills and the chapters that follow demonstrate that.

Additional Resources

Getting Started: Strategies for Introducing Media Literacy

www.medialit.org/getting-started-strategies-introducing-media-literacy-your-school-or-district

Introduction to Media Literacy

http://opi.mt.gov/pdf/TobaccoEd/IntroMediaLiteracy.pdf

Media Literacy Teaching Manual

www.alaska-ipc.org/documents/media_literacy_manual.pdf

LESSON 2

Close Reading and What It Means for Media Literacy

Background

The Common Core Standards call for students to become detectives: learning how to observe closely, locate evidence, look for clues, and ask the right questions. But today many students don't ask questions at all.

In my work as a media literacy consultant, I like to use media texts (and youth media) as the jumping-off point to get students asking questions.

A photograph from the morning's news can be coupled with the question "what do you see?" A snippet from a movie can be used to teach the language of film by asking "why do you think the director put the camera there?" A magazine cover featuring the latest celebrity can be used to get students to recognize layout, design, color, font, facial expression, body language, and much more.

As I travel around the United States conducting professional development workshops with teachers, I continually hear the same refrain: our students tend to believe everything they see, read, and hear in the media and on the Internet. Apparently many educators have not yet been trained to use materials from the news and popular media as catalysts to critical inquiry. Many are uncomfortable with the idea, in fact.

Close reading of print is something that is taught in colleges of education and in professional development sessions, but close reading of non-print (radio, photography, film, video) "texts" is seldom part of this professional learning process.

That's unfortunate because, as we all know, our students are very much drawn to this kind of media. It surrounds them. And because many now carry mobile phones or e-tablets with them, they have their media close at hand all of the time.

Activity: Learning to Question Media Texts

One way to get started is to ask students to bring in a favorite photo, magazine, advertisement, or movie. There are many ways to use these texts in a classroom activity or exercise. Depending on the media text, a variety of questions can be posed.

In media literacy education, these general questions are most often recommended. They make an excellent poster for the media literacy-savvy classroom (see also www.frankwbaker.com/KeyQuestions0001.jpg):

- who created/produced the message?
- why was this message created: what is its purpose?
- how was the message disseminated/distributed?
- what audiences is this message designed to reach?
- what techniques are used to attract your attention?
- who or what was omitted from the message and why?
- who benefits from the message?

Getting students in the habit of questioning media texts helps them begin to become critical thinkers and viewers. Oftentimes one question leads to another and another. Unanswered questions often lead to research which can also be revealing (and skill-building).

Teaching tip: Help students use media language when questioning their favorite photo, ad, or movie. Media language "encompasses all the ways in which media text is constructed to communicate with an audience through verbal, visual, aural language (e.g. lighting, layout, shots, typography, images, sound)" (www.nzqa.govt.nz/nqfdocs/ncea-resource/achievements/2011/as90277.pdf). Just as you need to deconstruct an author's language when close reading a novel or article, you also need to deconstruct a media text by taking apart the "language" used (http://media-studies.tki.org.nz/Teaching-media-studies/Media-concepts/Close-reading).

Additional Resources

There are many more critical thinking/viewing questions. See the full list I created here:

www.frankwbaker.com/media_messages

Frank Baker's Close Reading of Media Messages website:

http://frankwbaker.com/mlc/close-reading-of-media-texts

What's Missing From That Media Message?

Background

I was prompted to write about this topic after I was quoted in a news story (www.hlntv.com/articles/2015/11/30/diversity-in-advertising-thank-the-millennials) about a decision by some advertisers to begin including persons with disabilities and same-sex couples in their marketing messages.

It seems that when the holidays were nearing that year, some larger companies decided it was a good idea to acknowledge these underrepresented groups as members of our society. I wondered: what took them so long?

Advertisers who do include underrepresented groups in their messages are hoping to appear more inclusive, not exclusive. At the same time, the increasing visibility of these groups may help more people come to accept them as "normal." It's clearly a business decision by companies: they're hoping that including these groups will also increase their bottom line.

Years ago, I asked my media literacy workshop audiences if they could name a major character in primetime TV who was confined to a wheelchair. At the time I could only think of one: Raymond Burr who played the detective "Ironside" (1967–75). More recently, the character Artie from the hit show *Glee* (2009–15) used a wheelchair. But outside of these two examples, we'd be hard-pressed to name others.

Many minority groups regularly call on the media to be more inclusive. The news/journalism community is constantly being urged to include more reporters of color on their staffs and to address more issues that directly relate to underrepresented groups. Politics shift and cultural pressures morph over time, but from a marketing perspective, consumers are always going to want to "see me" in the media they consume.

The Hollywood Example

In recent years, the Hollywood production community has come under criticism for its lack of diversity among those individuals both in front of and behind the camera (www.usatoday.com/story/life/movies/2015/11/15/spike-lee-calls-lack-hollywood-diversity-ridiculous-debbie-reynolds-gena-rowlands/75821848).

Actress Geena Davis spearheaded a campaign to increase the visibility of females in both TV and film (www.cnsnews.com/news/article/lauretta-brown/actress-geena-davis-theres-gender-inequality-every-segment-society). And the Ralph Bunche Center for African American Studies at UCLA publishes a revealing Hollywood Diversity Report every few years (the most recent report, which includes charts and graphs you can analyze with students, can be found at www.bunchecenter.ucla.edu/wp-content/uploads/2017/04/2017-Hollywood-Diversity-Report-2-21-17.pdf).

The protests, documentation, and conversation have had a measurable effect. In 2015, Academy of Motion Picture Arts and Sciences president Cheryl Boone Isaacs (the first African American and third woman to hold the office) announced a five-year plan to get Hollywood executives to hire a more racially diverse workforce. And the Oscar nominations announced in January 2017 (for work done in 2016) showed considerably more diversity than in previous years.

However, after the 2017 nominations were announced, USA Today reporter Maria Puente wondered in an opinion piece:

> Is this the start of a permanent shift in nomination diversity or just a temporary break from the same-old, same-old? Is it the result of the Academy of Motion Picture Arts and Sciences' recent efforts to diversify and expand its voting membership? Or is it the consequence of a powerful social-media campaign to shame Hollywood about the persistent lack of diversity in the industry and in those it chooses to nominate and honor with gold statuettes every year?
>
> (www.usatoday.com/story/life/movies/2017/01/24/oscar-diversity-more-than-black-or-white-latinos-asians-excluded/96951730)

Are your students aware of this controversy over diversity in Hollywood? Puente's story might make a good backgrounder for a class discussion about whether and why more diversity is a worthy goal.

The Importance of Seeing "Me" in Media

The problem becomes: *what if I don't see me in media?* Young people today look for individuals like themselves in their media. Seeing the "me" in media impacts their self-esteem and self-confidence. If they don't see themselves reflected in their media, it may send a message that they're not important or valued in the American culture.

This topic – who or what is omitted and why – is quintessential. Media literacy involves critical thinking and critical inquiry and most of all, asking questions. Questions to be considered include: who created the message; who is the audience; what techniques do producers use to get my attention; and what is omitted and why?

That last question is one many of us, including our students, never consider. And that's unfortunate, because what you don't see, read, or hear might just be as important as what you do. (Why do you think car advertisers omit the miles per gallon or the price; why do pizza makers not reveal how much sodium is in one slice; why do car insurance ads not reveal their annual rates?)

What's being omitted is a question that can be broadly applied as our students expand their media awareness. Thinking about such omissions, I recently created a page on my Media Literacy Clearinghouse website titled "What You See and What You Don't" (www.frankwbaker.com/mlc/what-you-see). I divided the webpage into sections that include pop culture, the news, politics, advertising, and more. Here are a few examples that you can use with your students.

Activity 1: What You Don't See in This Photo

In 1943, landscape photographer Ansel Adams snapped a photo of a baseball game in California (see Figure 1.1). It's an impressive photograph looking out onto the baseball field with the beautiful mountain range in the background. But, as I like to remind my audiences, every photo has a story behind it. How many of us take the time to ask: what else is going on; what's outside the frame?

The detail that is revealing here is: Adams snapped this picture while he was staying at the Manzanar War Relocation Camp, a Japanese-American Internment Camp. Ask students: Does knowing that change the way you feel about the image?

Activity 2: Does the Celebrity Really Look Like This?

A popular celebrity is featured on the cover of a magazine. She appears perfect. But what most of us never consider is: what was done in the hours leading up to the shoot (lighting, makeup, etc.) and the hours after it (e.g., Photoshop), to make her look flawless? Today, there are many websites

Figure 1.1 Ansel Adams: Baseball game at Manzanar War Relocation Center, Owens Valley, California, 1943

(Source: https://commons.wikimedia.org/wiki/File:Ansel_Adams,_Baseball_game_at_Manzanar,_1943.jpg)

and blogs that take pride in showing audiences what a celebrity looked like before and after the use of digital alteration software (which may actually shrink arms as well as soften skin blemishes).

Media Link

Here's an image from a collection at the Uberhumor.com website showing an editor's Photoshop notes and the result:

http://uberhumor.com/celebrities-before-and-after-photoshop-30-pictures

Another example offered a before-and-after view of Faith Hill, posing for a Redbook magazine cover:

http://frankwbaker.com/mlc/redbook-magazine-faith-hill-cover

These are just two examples, but there are hundreds. Everyday media messages pass through our radar screens, and unfortunately many of us don't take the time to stop and consider: who sent this message and why am I seeing this or what might they not want me to know?

Many of us see only the final media product: a magazine, TV show, movie, videogame, etc. We don't often learn how it was made. But that's changing. Every media production involves many behind-the-scenes decisions and techniques that we're often not privileged to experience. That's why engaging young people in media production is so advantageous – it demonstrates the importance of process, collaboration, design, and technique that go into a final production.

1. Find several before-and-after images on the Internet. Look for diverse examples (not just celebrity models having their bodies enhanced). At Google Images, try a search string like: *photoshopped* [celebrities] or [fashion ads] or [food ads before and after]. Or a string like "what's missing from this picture?" Here's an interesting find at Upworthy of an Ikea ad doctored for Saudi Arabian audiences: www.upworthy.com/spot-the-difference-whats-missing-from-this-ikea-catalog-in-saudi-arabia.
2. Have students examine each before and after, then identify and discuss what's been changed. Why did the publishers of each image make the changes they did?

    - The more students begin to appreciate that a production might leave something critical on the cutting room floor – whether it's underrepresented groups, important information, or physical imperfections – the sooner they'll start down the road to becoming truly media-literate, 21st-century producers and learners.

Additional Resources

On my "Is Seeing Believing?" webpage (http://frankwbaker.com/mlc/is-seeing-believing), you'll find a host of other topics and readings related to the digital manipulation of images.

Also visit my Close Reading The Media website:

www.closereadingthemedia.org

September

The new fall TV season kicks off every September, and the media is always full of stories about which new series might be hits and which ones might not attract the desired audience. The ones that draw the fewest audiences will likely be canceled. All of this is tied to advertising, a topic that I explore in this chapter. (Be sure to be on the lookout for Advertising Age's latest data on those TV programs which command the most dollars for a 30-second ad. It's usually published in late September, after the new fall shows have premiered.)

September is also a key time for election season and political advertising at the local and national level. I've included a lesson on examining the political announcement, and one on truth vs propaganda in political ads.

LESSON 4

Unraveling the Messages in TV Advertising

Background

We know our students love to watch television, even if that "watching" isn't always in front of the actual TV these days. I really enjoy the fall season, when all of the new shows are unveiled (and the older ones return) and the competition starts: we begin to see which programs will survive and which ones won't.

I also like this time of year because that's when the audience determines which TV programs/series will command the highest price for a 30-second commercial. It's a no-brainer really: the larger the viewing audience (the more eyeballs), the more money the TV networks can charge advertisers.

And there's plenty of money involved. Companies are spending billions of dollars on television advertising to swing us toward their products and services. It's no exaggeration to say that your students' favorite TV shows could not have gotten "on the air" if it weren't for plentiful commercials. (The exceptions are PBS and premium commercial-free cable networks, like HBO, which have their own contributed or paid income streams.)

Do your students know how TV shows get on the air? The annual rite of pitching new TV shows to advertisers, known as "upfronts," occurs every spring, but probably gets little attention from educators (http://frankwbaker.com/mlc/understanding-tv-upfront).

Every September, Advertising Age (www.adage.com), the periodical of the ad/marketing industry, publishes an annual list of what it calls the "priciest" shows of a particular season. Here's a sample from 2016–17 (Table 2.1). You can see the full list here: http://adage.com/article/news/tv-ad-pricing-chart/305899. Three of the top four shows were all about sports, including NBC's Sunday Night Football, where a 30-second commercial cost an average of $673,664.

The Advertising Age story also highlights the "comeback" of Gray's Anatomy, which slipped from the top 10 in 2010. The show ended the 2015–16 season "as ABC's No. 1 series and the No. 2 returning broadcast drama in the all-important 18-to-49 demographic."

Table 2.1 Top priciest shows on broadcast for advertisers

1.	Sunday Night Football (NBC)	$673,664
2.	Thursday Night Football (CBS)	$522,910
3.	Thursday Night Football (NBC)	$486,695
4.	Empire (FOX)	$437,100
5.	The Big Bang Theory (CVS)	$289,136

Source: Adage.com

We should welcome opportunities to meet students where they are. We know they watch TV and they discuss the characters, plots, etc. So here is just another way to engage them.

In 2016, NBC's "Sunday Night Football" broadcast commanded the highest price for a 30-second commercial ($673,664), up from $603,000 in 2014. It's a breathtaking sum for one spot lasting a fraction of a minute. And why does it cost that much? Because more people are tuned into NBC at that time than to any other TV show on network or cable.

It's not only sports that command high prices. The drama "Empire" (FOX) came in at #4 on AdAge's survey, costing $437,100, down some from 2014's $497,364 per spot. (Empire came in #2 in 2014 – the first drama series to rate so high in a number of years – but lost ground when the networks took over Thursday Night Football.)

Many cable series (e.g., AMC's "Walking Dead") and situation comedies, also known as sitcoms (which are highly rated), have also been able to charge advertisers steep rates. (Visit this AdAge story and you'll find an interactive tool that will fascinate students, as they pull up trend data about their favorite shows: http://adage.com/article/news/tv-ad-pricing-chart/305899.)

As I always remind the audiences in my workshops, television has a first name: "Commercial." One of the key concepts in media literacy is that all media are businesses designed to make money. If the media doesn't make money, it ceases to exist. (TV shows which fail to maintain a large enough audience in the right demographics get canceled.)

So those advertisers who've spent lots of money to advertise on TV don't just sit back and watch the shows they advertise on. They also pay careful attention to the ratings. It is the ratings that measure how many eyeballs are watching each week. (For more about teaching with and about ratings, see my website "Math in the Media," www.frankwbaker.com/mlc/math-media.)

Television, with its plentiful data, offers one excellent way for students to understand the connections between the entertainment media they are served and the advertising/marketing engine that drives the entertainment economy.

Common Core Connections

Many educators I know teach with and about advertising. Before Common Core, ads were taught as part of the "techniques of persuasion." Now many teachers are positioning advertising as "argument," an important CCSS element. The wiki site "Teaching Pathos and Advertising as Argument" (http://creativeoutlet.wikispaces.com/1.+Teaching+Pathos+and+Advertising+as+Argument) offers some guidance with examples and lesson ideas.

The following Common Core standards might also be helpful in aligning media literacy lessons with key teaching goals:

> *W. 9–10.1.a.* Introduce precise claim(s), distinguish the claim(s) from alternate or opposing claims, and create an organization that establishes clear relationships among claim(s), counterclaims, reasons, and evidence.
>
> *W. 9–10.1.b.* Develop claim(s) and counterclaims fairly, supplying evidence for each while pointing out the strengths and limitations

Activity: Engage Students with TV's Real Purpose

1. Locate the 2016 AdAge story "TV Ad Pricing Chart" (http://adage.com/article/news/tv-ad-pricing-chart/305899). The chart *How Much For a 30-Second TV Spot?* is interactive and students will be highly engaged if they can access it on Internet devices. However, it's also possible to copy and distribute it as a student handout.
2. Have students identify all of the various genres represented in the AdAge annual survey results (handout). That should include sitcom, drama (hospital, detective, police, etc.), sci-fi, horror, variety, news, comedy, late night, reality, etc. Which ones command the highest ad costs; the lowest? Why do you think those genres attract large audiences? Which genres account for the most in the list; the least?
3. Assuming your students' favorite TV genre is reality, ask them to discuss and identify the appeal of reality. (Another interesting discussion: how real is "reality TV?") Ask them to locate all of the "reality" television programs in the survey. What networks broadcast reality TV? Why do some reality TV programs air more than one night in a week? Which night of the week seems to attract the largest audiences?

4. Have your students look at all of the various genres that are broadcast on the same night at the same time. For example, at 8 pm on a weeknight you might find a crime drama on one network, a sitcom on another, and a reality TV show on a third. Which program commands the highest ad price?
5. Have students contact the sales managers of local TV stations and cable operators. Have them inquire about the various ad rates charged to car dealers and other local advertisers who want to position their spots inside popular prime-time TV shows or shows like "Wheel of Fortune" and "Jeopardy." Task them with creating an infographic showing local ad rates.
6. Ask students to assume the role of a local advertiser. (That could be anything from a car dealer to a tire store to a jewelry store to a toy store.) Ask them to speculate which TV show(s) would be the best match for them to reach their target demographic. You might even assign students the task of watching a specific TV show over the course of a week, making a list of all of the advertisers on that show.

> of both in a manner that anticipates the audience's knowledge level and concerns.
>
> *W. 9–10.1.c.* Use words, phrases, and clauses to link the major sections of the text, create cohesion, and clarify the relationships between claim(s) and reasons, between reasons and evidence, and between claim(s) and counterclaims.
>
> *W. 9–10.1.e.* Provide a concluding statement or section that follows from and supports the argument presented.
>
> Advertising also plays a role in the teaching standards for Social Studies, Economics, Art, and Health, to name just a few.

Media Literacy and Beyond

As you can see, using TV as a jumping-off point, educators can teach about genre, math, demographics, economics, media ownership, and, of course, advertising.

Television and TV commercials are not going away, despite "cord cutting" (the practice of forgoing a cable or satellite TV subscription in favor of an alternative Internet-based service). In fact, almost every digital device has the ability to deliver live TV today. While network television advertising still dominates, new thinking about TV demographics is quickly emerging and complicating the picture.

Wherever all this takes us, there's no question that entertainment producers will continue to be after your students' eyeballs. Media literacy education encourages the kind of critical thinking and questioning that encourages an alert and thoughtful society.

Additional Resources

Advertising from TV to Internet: An Industry History

www.investopedia.com/articles/investing/022515/advertising-tv-internet-industry-history.asp

The State of Traditional TV: Updated with Q3 2016 Data

www.marketingcharts.com/television/are-young-people-watching-less-tv-24817

The New TV Demographics: The 'Ads' and 'Ad-Nots' (includes a brief history of television advertising)

http://venturebeat.com/2014/11/06/the-new-tv-demographics-the-ads-and-ad-nots

Sneaky Ads: How Commercials Are Hidden Everywhere

www.cbc.ca/news/business/sneaky-ads-how-commercials-are-hidden-everywhere-1.3378150

LESSON 5

Examining the Political Announcement

Background

In my book, *Political Campaigns & Political Advertising: A Media Literacy Guide,* I observed that politicians need the media, and media companies and reporters need politicians. It's a two-way street: the politician depends on media coverage to communicate his or her message to potential voters; the media benefits both in terms of audience and from campaign advertising that boosts its bottom line.

As a media educator, I want to help today's media-saturated students realize the lengths that political consultants will go to get (and keep) our attention now and in the future. *Never before had the visual message been more important than it was in the 2016 Presidential race.* Here are some examples.

Three candidates (GOP senators Ted Cruz, Rand Paul, and Marco Rubio) chose specific physical locations for their presidential announcements. Cruz, for instance, chose to announce, as the Washington Post reported, "at a landmark of the American evangelical movement, Liberty University."

Democrat Hillary Clinton elected to bypass the physical announcement entirely, taking her message to the voters via a YouTube video (http://youtu.be/0uY7gLZDmn4): one that appears to be a two-minute-long campaign commercial.

The Washington Times accurately predicted (www.washingtontimes.com/news/2015/apr/5/ted-cruz-marco-rubio-launch-2016-white-house-bids-) that other candidates would

> pick their own symbolic locations as the campaign enters the beginning of the scripted period, when what consultants and talking heads call "optics" becomes paramount, and when, how and where a candidate speaks can be even more important than what is actually said.

The Times quoted Daniel Schill, associate professor in the School of Communication Studies at James Madison University, who said: "Candidates will strategically select locations that articulate the themes of the campaign and reinforce the issues and arguments that will serve as their rationale for running."

Schill, author of *Stagecraft and Statecraft: Advance and Media Events in Political Communication*, told *The Times* that "candidates usually kick off their candidacies in places that hold personal or symbolic meaning." Schill calls such locations "sacred sites."

Former political campaign consultant Josh King has coined the word "polioptics" to describe the stagecraft and choreography at work whenever candidates make appearances that will inevitably be covered by the media.

> The creation, production and distribution of image to persuade audiences in one direction or another is happening all around us, from Washington to Beijing and every place in between. It is a fundamental driver of politics, entertainment, marketing and popular culture. It is ever-changing and endlessly fascinating, from the roots of influence through image to the technology-driven developments of today.
>
> (www.polioptics.com)

And, let's not forget, it is the media (broadcast and social) that will be communicating these crafted messages and visuals to us, the potential voter, via tomorrow's news. This is true whether candidates appear physically or virtually. (This US News story, www.usnews.com/news/blogs/run-2016/2015/04/20/hillary-clinton-ted-cruz-create-biggest-splashes-with-2016-announcements, reported on the media response to the first wave of presidential candidate announcements.)

Politics, Visual Literacy, and Learning Standards

Politics has capitalized on media since the invention of the printing press, but in the 21st century it is a decidedly more visual experience. More people are working in the visual and design fields than ever before, whether creating an enticing pitch for pizza or a compelling vision of the next President. So, visual literacy – the ability to deconstruct, analyze, comprehend, and question what we are shown – is a critical skill in modern society. In the world of politics, this fact is reinforced when we see that university professors like Daniel Schill are focusing their scholarship on political optics.

The importance of visual literacy is also acknowledged by teaching standards. The Common Core calls for students to become better discerners of persuasive messaging by engaging in "close reading" of both print and non-print sources. And in a 2013 Position Statement on Technology, the National Council on the Social Studies made reference to the importance of teaching with and about political media: "Given social studies educators' expertise with sourcing historical evidence, critically analyzing political messages, and drawing inferences from GIS data, they are well equipped to further students' media literacy and related skills" (www.socialstudies.org/positions/technology).

Teaching Students to Analyze Visual Images in Political Settings

The first and perhaps most important feature of media literacy is representation. How are products – or in this case, candidates – being presented? In the political arena, consultants go to work deciding how to use colors, symbols, camera angles, and music to appeal to the news consumer. After deciding on a setting, they will design the stage and all of the other trappings to take full advantage of the camera. Everything is pre-planned and carefully orchestrated.

Then comes the "reveal." The candidate (and often his or her family members) emerge wearing smiles and brightly colored or accented clothes. From the moment a candidate walks onto the stage until they finish their speech and exit the location, viewers are experiencing a highly produced political show. So how do we get students to deconstruct this event?

Activity 1: The Staging of Political Announcements

1. When working with students, we might take an example like the popular image of Senator Ted Cruz and family on the day of his April 2015 announcement (see Media Link box on the next page for photo URL). With students I prefer to use images without captions and guide them through a close reading exercise which starts with the question: *What do you see?* But for our purposes, I am including the captions as provided by the photojournalists working for the news organizations.

The following questions might be used to guide student thinking and understanding:

- What is the setting? Why do you think that location was chosen?
- What is prominent in the image? What is missing?
- Where is the camera positioned that took this image? Why do you think it has been placed there? What is shown and what is not?
- What color or colors and symbols are visible?
- Is the candidate's name, slogan, or other message visible? If so, what is it?

You might also ask students, "Do you think this was rehearsed?" Then show them an image taken before the event, showing the Cruz family practicing (see Media Link box below).

2. Finally, have students consider another image, from the *New York Magazine* website: Senator Rand Paul used a Louisville, Kentucky hotel as the location of his announcement. Return to the previous questions and have students consider them as you look at the image of Senator Paul. Compare the Cruz and Paul images and have students look for both similarities and differences.

Media Link

1. Ted Cruz image: http://frankwbaker.com/mlc/ted-cruz-paul-rand.
2. Cruz family practicing: https://img.washingtonpost.com/rf/image_1484w/2010-2019/Wires/Images/2015-03-22/AP/GOP_2016_Cruz-0c4f0.jpg.
3. Rand Paul image: http://frankwbaker.com/mlc/ted-cruz-paul-rand.

Activity 2: Other Ways to Analyze a Candidate's Campaign

Take a look at these additional ideas and suggestions for how to engage your students in critical thinking, visual literacy, and media literacy during a campaign season.

1. Assign students to conduct an evaluation of several political candidates' websites. How is each website designed to take advantage of colors, symbols, and more? How does each candidate integrate social media into the website? (Even in the political off-season it's possible to find sites for candidates who are "testing the waters." And for now-defunct campaign sites, try searching the Internet Archive Wayback Machine: https://archive.org/web.)
2. Task your students with watching one or more of the candidates' TV commercials and have them begin to notice how persuasive these messages can be. (Many past ads can be found on YouTube.) It will be important for students to recognize the techniques being used. Can they understand how the type of music, for example, might provoke an emotional response for the audience? On page 30 of this book, you'll find a worksheet for analyzing and deconstructing a candidate's commercials. A downloadable version can also be found online at www.frankwbaker.com/mlc/political-ad-analyzing-worksheet.

3. Have your students consider the online evaluations of candidate claims in ads and speeches. FactCheck.org and PolitiFact.com are two of the longest operating watchdog sites. The Annenberg Foundation, which supports FactCheck.org, has also launched FlackCheck.org to promote "political literacy." (During election season watch your local media – newspapers, TV stations – as many conduct their own ad-watch analyses as the election draws closer.)
4. The lesson plans on the Living Room Candidate (website www.livingroomcandidate.org/lessons) are also worth considering, as are the resources on this McDougal-Littell textbook website: www.classzone.com/books/lnetwork_gr10/page_build.cfm?content=analyz_media&ch=29.
5. Listen to an episode of Polioptics Radio. More than 150 episodes, featuring professional political consultants and journalists, are listed on the Polioptics website (see list in right margin of the home page). For example, Episode 9 (www.polioptics.com/2011/05/polioptics-radio-on-p-o-t-u-s-%E2%80%94-broadcast-episode-9-%E2%80%94-howard-wolfson-deputy-mayor-of-new-york-city) features guests Howard Wolfson, a Hillary Clinton presidential campaign advisor in 2008, and Kevin Sullivan, former communications director for President George W. Bush.

During any major election season, a vast flood of images will be published and thousands of videos will be uploaded to video-sharing sites. All of this is designed to keep us interested and get our attention. If students are more critical and possess the necessary media literacy skills, they will be better equipped to see through the spin and fluff that have become part of the American political landscape.

Additional Resources

For background on the persuasion techniques used in ads, look at the resources on my media and politics website:

http://frankwbaker.com/mlc/media-politics

Political Advertising Analysis Worksheet

Directions: Use the space under each item to take notes on the ad you're analyzing.

WHERE? the ad was seen/heard (social media, TV, radio)	WHEN? the ad was seen/heard (social media, TV, radio)	AUDIENCE who is targeted?	TYPE see list below	SPONSOR (who paid for the message?) candidate, party, Super PAC	IMAGES* see list below	SOUNDS* see list below	TECHNIQUES* used

Types of Political Ads:

Negative – One candidate portrays the other in an unfavorable light.
Warm and Fuzzy – Candidates make the viewer feel good about the country or his/her campaign.
Biography and Vision – Candidates emphasize their life or "vision" for America.
Humorous – Candidates elicit a laugh or smile from the viewer.
Scary – Candidates evoke images of fear (usually combined with a negative ad).
Advocacy – Candidates advocate for/against a certain position(s) on an issue/person.
Trust – Candidates seek to convince voters that they are someone they can trust to lead them during challenging times.

* Things to pay attention to:

Colors Superimposed Words Props Code Words People Music Symbols Clothing

*Techniques: Appeals to fear/prejudice; bandwagon; card stacking; fancy figures; flattery/insincerity; glittering generality; image transfer; loaded words; name calling; negativity; inferences as facts; quotes out of context; repetition; rumor mongering; warm and fuzzy image; catchy words/phrases

LESSON 6

Truth vs Propaganda in Political Ads

Background

If you lived in Iowa, New Hampshire, or South Carolina, you could not have escaped the 2016 presidential campaign ads that inundated broadcast and cable stations.

In 2012, I wrote a backgrounder on political TV ads which are slickly produced and highly persuasive. Years later, even with a big surge in social media, television continues to be the medium that reaches the largest number of potential voters.

Media Link

Here's a political cartoon to show students on TV campaign ads:

http://frankwbaker.com/mlc/hockey-editorial-cartoon

Yes, even in this multimedia Internet age with social media at everyone's fingertips, advertising by politicians on television has not gone out of style.

A group that monitors campaign advertising reported in 2014 that the amount spent on media ads during the midterm federal elections would top the $1 billion mark. That's a lot of money. But it was dwarfed by 2016 spending on presidential and other federal elections, with estimates as high as $7 billion. And who are the beneficiaries of all of this cash? The media outlets and their parent companies mostly.

Now here is something most students don't know: campaign ads are considered "free speech," and thus cannot be edited, censored, or blocked by media broadcasters. Given this amount of leeway, political candidates will (and do) say anything (even outright lies) in their ads.

So how are students supposed to know what to believe? Advertising surrounds us and these persuasive political messages ramp up around primary and general election time in every year candidates run for office. If students aren't educated to see through these slickly produced commercials, they're bound to believe much of what they see and hear.

When we teach our students to carefully dissect these types of ads, we help them to develop the kind of critical thinking and viewing skills that produce savvy if skeptical citizens.

The Common Core English language arts standards recognize advertising messages as "argument" – emphasizing a focus on purposes, techniques, and audiences. The National Social Studies standards also make references to the evolving role of media in society as well as how advertising and social media have become key parts of the political process.

With a multitude of ads being posted on YouTube, as well as being broadcast on television and cable, accessing these messages for teaching purposes is easier than ever. Most of these ads are 30 seconds (or less) in length, so they're perfect for playback, close reading, analysis, and deconstruction.

Most campaign ads meet the common definition of *propaganda*: "Information, especially of a biased or misleading nature, used to promote or publicize a particular political cause or point of view." Sad to say, there may be no source of misinformation riper for investigation by your students as they study persuasion and argument.

A non-profit website, the Political Ad Archive (http://politicaladarchive.org), was established by a group of foundation funders to provide "a searchable, viewable, and shareable online archive of 2016 political TV ads, married with trustworthy fact-checking and reporting." It's a great resource for media literacy teachers. For stories focused on key

Common Core Connections

Before Common Core, teachers might have used these types of ads to teach persuasion techniques or persuasive writing. The CCSS prefers the term "argument" or argumentative writing. (Here's an interesting post considering the differences: www.vriuvm.org/uncategorized/persuasive-vs-argument-writing.)

Several Common Core standards are relevant here:

> *W. 9–10.1.a.* Introduce precise claim(s), distinguish the claim(s) from alternate or opposing claims, and create an organization that establishes clear relationships among claim(s), counterclaims, reasons, and evidence.
>
> *W. 9–10.1.b.* Develop claim(s) and counterclaims fairly, supplying evidence for each while pointing out the strengths and limitations of both in a manner that anticipates the audience's knowledge level and concerns.
>
> *W. 9–10.1.c.* Use words, phrases, and clauses to link the major sections of the text, create cohesion, and clarify the relationships between claim(s) and reasons, between reasons and evidence, and between claim(s) and counterclaims.

political advertising events during the 2016 campaign, try this *New York Times* collection: www.nytimes.com/interactive/2016/us/politics/presidential-campaign-election-ads-2016.html?ref=politics.

> *W. 9–10.1.e.* Provide a concluding statement or section that follows from and supports the argument presented.
>
> *L. 9–10. 4.a.* Use context (e.g., the overall meaning of a sentence, paragraph, or text; a word's position or function in a sentence) as a clue to the meaning of a word or phrase.

Activity 1: Questions to Ask About Political Ads

For more than 15 years, I have maintained a media and politics website, www.frankwbaker.com/mlc/media-politics, which is designed to provide educators with resources and activities to teach with and about the relentless stream of 30-second political spots broadcast during campaign season.

Because these fast-paced political commercials go by so quickly, it will be necessary to play back ads more than once to engage your students in "active, critical viewing skills." One way to do that is to consider using my Political Advertising Analysis Worksheet, shown in Lesson 5 on page 30. Here are some questions you could use as starting points:

1. Who creates these ads?
2. What are the most common argument techniques used in these ads?
3. Do those clichéd techniques actually work?
4. How much does it cost to buy time on television?
5. Why is there a large discrepancy between what a candidate pays for time and what a Super PAC pays?
6. Who benefits when campaigns buy time on TV?
7. How much money was spent on political advertising during the 2016 election cycle?
8. What are some of the TV programs I watch where I am most likely to see these ads?

On this web page, www.frankwbaker.com/mlc/questions-for-students-to-consider-about-political-campaign-ads, I provide resources students can pursue to find answers to most of these questions. After some discussion centered on these questions, students can analyze some real political ads.

My advice is to show the ad first with no instruction. Next, distribute the worksheet. Assign students one of the columns. Ask them to pay careful attention. Play the ad again. Have them share their observations.

Most of us, including our students, watch these ads passively. The worksheet activity engages them in active viewing – tasking our students with deconstructing the ads based on many factors: images, sounds, and much more.

Additionally, you might want to make sure your students understand some of the vocabulary used at this time of year. Do your students understand what *dark money* is or what comprises a *Super PAC*, or the importance of the *Citizens United vs Federal Elections Commission* Supreme Court ruling, which held that "Political spending is a form of protected speech under the First Amendment, and the government may not keep corporations or unions from spending money to support or denounce individual candidates in elections" (www.scotusblog.com/case-files/cases/citizens-united-v-federal-election-commission)?

Activity 2: Engaging Students in Political Ad Scriptwriting

What would students say if they could represent candidates through media advertising? Find out by trying this activity:

1. Assign each student (or group of students) to one of the 2016 presidential candidates or other candidates of your choice.
2. Next, have them choose (or assign them) one of the campaign issues.
3. Ask them to research their candidate's position on that issue. (This research could include the candidate's own website, their speeches, or other resources such as "On the Issues": www.ontheissues.org/default.htm.)
4. Using a simple 30-second script template (www.frankwbaker.com/blank_script_form.htm), have them write a commercial for their candidate. Students might look at the 2012 Obama TV ad "Children" and its audio transcript to see how words and visuals are blended: https://parc.umd.edu/past-parc-projects-2/2012-ad-analyses/obama-for-president-children. For practice, they might fill in the template by deconstructing this ad.
5. They should also consider: who is the audience for my ad, and what TV program or series will I buy time on to broadcast my ad to the target audiences I want to reach?

Activity 3: So What Can We Believe?

For several years now, newspapers and broadcast agencies have started to run "fact check" columns on what politicians say in their ads. (Check your local newspaper or TV station to determine if they're offering this service.)

These journalism organizations, which are attached to commercial enterprises, realized at some point that after taking millions of dollars for advertising (and not challenging the veracity of the spots), it was their responsibility to investigate everything in the ads and report their findings. So fact checking was born.

The "fact checkers" can't block the advertising, but they can break down the words, images, and claims *in* the ads and report on what they find. And it's not just ads; some groups investigate speeches and more.

Students could be challenged not only to watch a candidate's ad, but also to investigate the claims in the ad. And part of that research should include a review of the "fact checkers."

Here are some places to start:

FactCheck.org (Annenberg Public Policy Center)

Politifact.com (*Tampa (FL) Times* newspaper)

WashingtonPost Factchecker: www.washingtonpost.com/news/fact-checker

FlackCheck.org (A Project of Annenberg Classroom) uses parody and humor to debunk false political advertising.

Political campaign seasons offer teachable moments. When we provide students with critical thinking questions and active viewing skills, we guarantee that they will watch the blizzard of political advertising differently. Thomas Jefferson famously said that the health of our democracy depends on an informed electorate. Engaging students in these political messages, and pulling back the curtain on the techniques used to sway viewers, is just another step in their becoming informed citizens.

Additional Resources

Political Advertising Resource Center (University of Maryland) – Resources include numerous political campaign ads with video, audio transcript, and analysis:

https://parc.umd.edu

What Works in a Campaign Commercial? Ad Executives Offer Their Take (*New York Times*, October 28, 2012):

www.nytimes.com/2012/10/29/us/politics/what-works-in-a-campaign-commercial-ad-executives-offer-their-take.html

October

The Annual Media Literacy Week (which falls in October or November) is designed to build awareness of media literacy and its role not only in education but also outside the classroom. In Lesson 7 that follows, you'll see how you can help students spread awareness about the importance of media literacy.

October is also a key time for political debates, so I've included a lesson on how to analyze them. And finally, there is a lesson on the all-important topic of helping students spot fake news.

LESSON 7

Media Literacy Week

A Time to Remember Why Media Literacy Is So Important

Background

The news is filled with headlines that continue to demonstrate why teaching media literacy is more important than ever. For example, here's a headline from September 2015, referring to the practice of presenting sales material in "news-like" formats online:

> Most People Think Native Ads Are Real Articles – and They Later Feel Duped
>
> (www.ibtimes.com/most-people-think-native-ads-are-real-articles-they-later-feel-duped-study-2087024)

Native ads are vaguely disguised and frequently appear in news feeds and on other websites. Often times these "ads" are labeled, but despite that many people were fooled according to the study (https://contently.com/strategist/2015/09/08/article-or-ad-when-it-comes-to-native-no-one-knows) by the marketing firm Contently.

Media Link

Here's an example of a native ad in the *New York Times* that you can show students: https://paidpost.nytimes.com/netflix/women-inmates-separate-but-not-equal.html.

If ever there was a need for media literacy, this is evidence. An August 2015 headline:

> 2016 SATs Will Put Stronger Emphasis on Graphic Literacy
>
> (www.scientificamerican.com/article/2016-sats-will-put-stronger-emphasis-on-graphic-literacy)

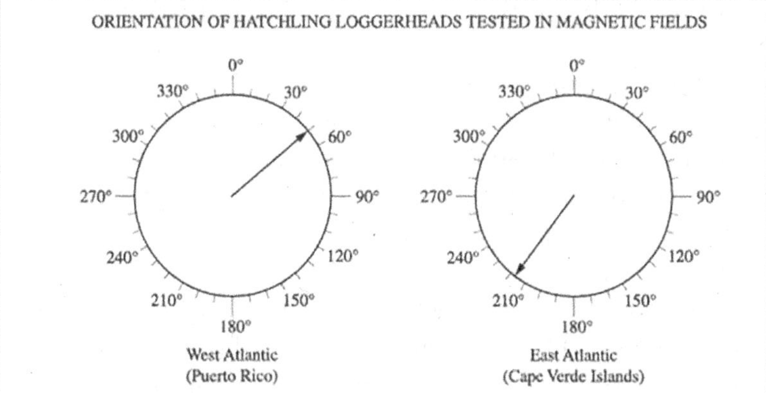

Adapted from Nathan Putman, Courtney Endres, Catherine Lohmann, and Kenneth Lohmann, "Longitude Perception and Bicoordinate Magnetic Maps in Sea Turtles." © 2011 by Elsevier Inc.

Figure 3.1 Image from test specifications for the redesigned SAT (p. 52)

The article acknowledges that more information is being conveyed visually and it's vital that today's students know how to interpret it. The article also notes that students who take the SAT college admissions test will be exposed to graphic literacy questions not only in math but also in the reading and writing portions of the test (see Figure 3.1). An executive of the College Board, which owns and publishes the SAT, says "being a literate consumer of that (kind of visual) information is valuable regardless of your career."

Are you using infographics or other visual displays of information with your students? Now might be a good time to start.

In a world where social media, music, television, and movies attract the attention of young people, we need to acknowledge that teaching about the media can no longer be ignored in the nation's classrooms.

Celebrate and Promote Media Literacy Week

The first week in November has been designated as Media Literacy Week (http://medialiteracyweek.us) by the National Association of Media Literacy Education (NAMLE). The week has been established to highlight the power of media literacy education and its important and relevant role in education today.

In its 2015 inaugural year, NAMLE celebrated those organizations and educators who take the time to demonstrate the importance of media literacy in a world where media dominate. Participating groups sponsor a variety of activities to bring attention to the issue. Educators can keep up with events by following @medialiteracyed on Twitter or NAMLE's Facebook page.

Every educator who uses images and videos in instruction should be interested in what media literacy aims to do. One of its objectives is to create "healthy skeptics" among those who consume media. Another objective is to turn "passive viewers" into "active, critical viewers." Additionally, media literacy aims to balance the analysis of media messages with the opportunity to engage students in creating their own media productions, thereby deepening their understanding of how it all works.

Some teachers tell me they don't have time to add another thing to their crowded plate. My response is: if you don't take the time, then you're not fully preparing your students to live and work in the 21st century.

Jim Burke, author of *The English Teacher's Companion* (3rd ed., 2007, Heinemann), referenced the importance of using popular culture in his chapter on media literacy: "Movies, advertisements, and all other visual media are tools teachers need to use, and media we must master if we are to maintain our credibility in the coming years."

But don't mistake media literacy as just the responsibility of the English teacher. In a study I conducted in 1999, elements of media literacy were also found in the teaching standards of Social Studies and Health. Today we can add Arts, Technology, Math, Science, and much more.

Media literacy education is now recognized and recommended by:

- The College Board;
- Partnership for 21st Century Skills;
- National Board of Professional Teaching Standards;
- National Council of Teachers of English;
- National Council for the Social Studies;
- Workskills 2020 Report;
- all these Media Literacy Week partners: http://medialiteracyweek.us/home/current-partners.

The introduction to the Common Core English language arts standards (http://medialiteracyweek.us/home/current-partners) makes reference to the importance of our students being able to analyze and produce both print and non-print messages. That's a direct reference to media literacy.

Activity: Get Students Involved in Media Literacy Week

Have students get involved in Media Literacy Week and promote the need for media literacy education among some different groups so they can learn about media literacy at a deeper level themselves.

1. Divide students into groups and have them choose one of the following audiences: 1. Peers; 2. Educators; 3. General public – civics groups, etc.
2. Have students decide what they will do to inform their chosen group about the importance of media literacy. For example, students could create a website that raises awareness; it could include data from their own schools about how much attention is given to media literacy and what evidence there is in research, etc. that more needs to be given. They could even include their own hashtag or social media campaign if applicable.
3. Have groups share their work with the class. Note: If you're able to start this project early in October, students could roll out their work during Media Literacy Week and families/community members could be invited to hear the presentations.

Additional Resources

NAMLE has a website featuring other ways teachers can get involved with colleagues or through class lessons: https://medialiteracyweek.us

Teach Students to Analyze Political Debates

Background

Political debates provide rich teaching opportunities in social studies, language arts, and media literacy. In addition to helping students understand the role of debates in our election process, using debates as a teaching tool will help them examine the candidates' use of language and word choice and observe the media's influence on both the debate process and the electorate.

The U.S. 2016 presidential campaign debates provided a wealth of dramatic moments, thwarted expectations, and unusual exchanges among candidates during both the primaries and the general election. These quadrennial events are by far the most viewed and scrutinized political debates in America.

But students may also have opportunities to view debates closer to home involving candidates for Congressional, state, and city/county offices, via local broadcasts, public television, and Internet sources. Searching out venues for students to observe and critique debates among political office seekers outside the presidential selection process can also help them broaden their understanding of electoral politics, campaigning techniques, and media's role in determining who will govern us.

In presidential debates and any other debates among candidates running for office, the core media literacy concepts and related questions are much the same:

1. All media are constructed. The way media events are put together has purpose. Who is responsible for creating the debate? Who decides the questions? How are audience members involved, if at all? Who is omitted from participation and why? What topics might be left out and why?
2. Media sources use language unique to the medium. Live debates depend on video and audio. How are visual symbols, sound effects, stagecraft, split-screen, and cutaways used and why?
3. Many media are created or hosted for commercial purposes. Who is the audience? Who benefits from these debates? Are they sponsored? Who are the advertisers? If there are no advertisers, who paid the costs of production?

In the activities that follow, we'll address many of these concepts and questions.

Activity 1: Preparing Students to Watch and Analyze a Debate

What do your students need to know before they watch a political debate? Simply taking notes is no longer sufficient. Students who plan to watch a debate should, ahead of time, learn the candidates' positions and prior statements on various topics. In the case of general election campaigns, reading news stories that analyzed primary debates would be helpful in gaining the "lay of the land."

- Students can research the candidates' positions using candidate websites.
- Ask students to choose three or four issues listed on the candidates' websites and present the pros and cons of each. Succinct summaries and arguments for and against many major national issues are available at ProCon.org. Local and state issues might be described and analyzed in local/state media sources, including editorial pages.
- Introduce and review debate-oriented glossary terms, like these at my website: http://frankwbaker.com/mlc/debate-glossary-page.
- If you have access to a debate club sponsor, you might invite the teacher to talk to students about different kinds of debates. One thing for students to keep in mind is that political debates are not debates in the classic sense.
    - A traditional debate is a formal, oral contest between two individuals or teams that present arguments to support opposing sides of a question (the pros and the cons). Such debates follow a set of rules so that participants can state their positions and challenge their opponents' views in a fair and orderly manner.
    - With few exceptions, American national and local election-year debates follow a Q-and-A format covering multiple topics. In the case of serial presidential debates, each may focus on a specific area, such as foreign policy. The rules of formal debate are not in play.
- Students may want to research the "rules of debate" for the particular campaign event they plan to observe. In the 2016 presidential debates between Clinton and Trump, moderators selected by the bipartisan Commission on Presidential Debates (established in the 1980s) determined topics and "enforced" debate protocols. If students are examining other political debates, how are they structured and who decided on the structure? See: www.nytimes.com/2016/09/03/business/presidential-debate-moderators-lester-holt-chris-wallace.html.

Activity 2: Viewing vs Listening

To sharpen the students' media literacy skills, consider doing the following activity: Ask for several volunteers who will only *listen* to a debate. They may find it carried by the local NPR station, or they may simply put a cover over the screen of their TV during the debate, leaving the sound on. Discuss the students' different perceptions based on whether they viewed or only listened to the debate. (See post-viewing discussion below.)

Activity 3: Watching the Debate

In any televised political debate there are two levels or types of viewing that can occur. One focuses on the content – the specific proposals and ideas offered by each candidate. The other looks at the non-content aspects of the debate, which include the television production techniques and the non-verbal cues ("body language") displayed by the candidates themselves.

Analysis of both types of viewing falls under the umbrella of media literacy. Students can take notes about either or both using a Media Literacy Analysis Worksheet I have tailored specifically for political debates between two candidates: See page 47 of this book, and you can access a downloadable version here: http://frankwbaker.com/mlc/debate-analysis-worksheet (if more candidates are involved, feel free to revise my format to suit your needs).

You might want to ask some students to track content and others to take notes about the non-content aspects (it can be difficult to pay attention to both at once).

Here's what to look for:

Content. What ideas or proposals, old or new, do the candidates present during the debate?

Production techniques. Where is the camera focused? Are there shots such as split-screen, or reaction shots of the other candidate or audience members? Is there music? What kind? When is it used? What does the stage look like? What colors are used in the background? How do these techniques affect the viewer's perception of the debate?

Candidates' language. Often, prior to the debate, candidates have gone after each other in speeches and in commercials. They may have resorted to name-calling or phrases that impugn their opponent's integrity. (In 2016, for example, Donald Trump repeatedly used the phrases "lyin' Hillary" and "crooked Hillary." Hillary Clinton called her opponent "unprepared" and some of his supporters "phobics.") Students should be aware of such prior language so they can listen for it during the debate.

Use of oppositional research. Candidates or their consultants may have done "oppositional research" to discover issues where their opponent is most vulnerable to criticism. Have students listen for examples of each candidate targeting vulnerabilities that they think will get the attention of voters.

Emotional language. Many candidates have certain emotional buzzwords or phrases that they like to use. For example, in the 2016 presidential debates, Trump frequently sprinkled his statements with superlatives, such as "tremendous." Clinton often made reference to "the American people" and the need to be "stronger together." During the debate, what emotional content might your students detect and what might those words reveal about the candidates?

Body language. Research has shown that a candidate's body language – facial expressions, gestures, voice tone, appearance (like rolled-up sleeves or color choices) – do as much to influence public reaction to the debates as what the candidates actually say. Students should "listen" to body language and note what they see.

Texas Tech and University of Arkansas researchers report that "False smiles, toothy smiles, eye blinks and darting eyes . . . are the expressions that appear in reaction shots, and in the moments that are replayed for days after the debates." All of this becomes evident during camera cutaways. When one candidate criticizes another, students should note whether the broadcaster cuts away to show us the reaction shot.

Media Link

Here's a 2012 example of a familiar political debate "split-screen" shot. While GOP candidate Mitt Romney is speaking, another shot of President Obama (right, listening and reacting) is seen on the same screen: http://frankwbaker.com/mlc/romney-obama-split-screen.

Activity 4: Conducting Post-Debate Analysis with Students

Students can use the notes from their Media Literacy Analysis Worksheet as they conduct some post-debate analysis. During the discussion, students might consider these questions, among others:

- In general, did the candidates answer the questions asked by the moderator, or did they use the time primarily to repeat statements that are part of their campaign rhetoric?
- How effective was the moderator in attempting to keep candidates "on topic"?
- What new information, if any, did students learn from or about either candidate?
- Discuss some or all of the sections of the Media Literacy Analysis Worksheet. How would students evaluate each candidate's overall performance in the debate? What differences in perception arise among students?
- How did viewing compare to only listening? Ask the "listeners" who avoided watching the visual broadcast which candidate came across as more informed or more eloquent. How do their perceptions compare with those who were "viewers"? How do they explain the differences?

Further Exploration: The Two-Party System

The two major political parties in the U.S. have evolved as a matter of tradition, but there is no law restricting the number of parties. In fact, many presidential races have included one or more third-party candidates. Ask students to research and discuss the role of parties other than the Republicans and Democrats in previous presidential campaigns. Why did historian Richard Hofstadler famously say that "Third parties are like bees. Once they have stung, they die"? (http://people.howstuffworks.com/10-third-party-presidential-candidates.htm.)

Third-party candidates are frequently left out of general election debates. For example, in 2016, the Commission on Presidential Debates determined that third-party candidates (Libertarian, Green) had not received enough support in polls to enable them to participate in the presidential debates. Do students think that's fair? How might a debate be different if third-party candidates participated? Might they be more issue-oriented?

Opportunities for Rich Learning Experiences

Presidential, federal, state, and local political debates all provide a portal through which students can explore a multitude of topics that are critically important in developing their media literacy skills and preparing them for a future role as voting citizens in a democracy.

Debate Analysis Worksheet

Things to Pay Attention To:	Candidate #1	Candidate #2
Setting What is the location? What do you know about it? Are logos for the sponsors prominently displayed? Look for examples of how colors, camera positions, and view framing (e.g., close-ups, side view, other angles) favor or hurt the candidate		
Rhetoric: Argument/Evidence What specific argument(s) and evidence does the candidate use to bolster his/her case on a specific topic?		
Rhetoric: Techniques of Persuasion Examples of candidates' use of glittering generalities, name-calling, emotional appeals, avoidance, etc. Did these examples help or hurt the candidate?		
Rhetoric: Content What new ideas/proposals did the candidate put forward, if any?		
Rhetoric: Favorite Phrases Examples of candidates' use of slogans and buzz words. Were they used effectively or not?		
Rhetoric: Rehearsed Responses Examples of candidates' use of prepared phrases or retorts that seem spontaneous. Were they used effectively or not?		
TV Cutaways/Reaction Shots Examples of non-verbal expressions, gesturing, and audience reactions seen during debate. What did you notice? Did these images help or hurt the candidates?		
Post-Debate Analysis Examples of horse-race words/phrases used by commentators, pundits, others. Did they favor a candidate? Examples of challenges to factual accuracy of candidates' claims. Were candidates' statements supported by facts?		

The time involved in pursuing these "live" learning opportunities is a worthwhile and even crucial investment in any student's civic and media literacy education.

Visit this page at the Media Literacy Clearinghouse for additional presidential debate resources: http://frankwbaker.com/mlc/resources-watch-presidential-debate.

Note: My colleague Karen Zill, a freelance writer based in Washington, D.C., co-wrote the original article upon which this activity is based. Karen's work includes film discussion guides, teacher guides for public television programs, and essays and articles on media literacy.

LESSON 9

Students Need Help Detecting Fake News

Background

Fake news. Alternate facts. Click bait. Parodies posing as real journalism. Today, media consumers are being routinely exposed to *deliberately* manipulated headlines in the news. And while some will argue that false or exaggerated new stories are as old as journalism itself, today's instant communication tools – email, blogging, and social media like Facebook, Twitter and SnapChat – make it possible to compose, publish, and sway mass opinion in the time it once took to ink a press.

And lots of us are fooled, including our students, because we don't stop and question the source of the information. All too often we're anxious to forward "news" and we click before making sure that the news isn't wrong or deceptive.

In a speech in Germany, shortly after the 2016 U.S. general election, President Obama said:

> If we are not serious about facts and what's true and what's not, and particularly in an age of social media when so many people are getting their information in sound bites and off their phones, if we can't discriminate between serious arguments and propaganda, then we have problems.

The Rise of "Fake News"

The discussion about "fake news" intensified in the weeks before and after the 2016 election of Donald Trump, including a disputed BuzzFeed report suggesting that fake political news dominated real news in social media during the campaign. Other articles told stories of fake-news creators in foreign countries attempting to influence the U.S. election.

One former fake-news producer in the U.S., Paul Horner, claimed to the *Washington Post* that he had "unintentionally" swayed the election by creating fake stories that appeared to be coming from major media companies, such as ABC and CNN, and disseminating them across Facebook. Examples included stories saying "that Obama was invalidating the election results and banning the national anthem at sporting events."

"Honestly, people are definitely dumber," Horner told the *Post*. "They just keep passing stuff around. Nobody fact-checks anything anymore ... It's real scary. I've never seen anything like it." (www.slate.com/blogs/the_slatest/2016/11/17/purveyor_of_fake_news_says_he_targeted_trump_supporters_influenced_election.html.)

A January 2017 report from a pair of researchers at Stanford and New York University seemed to validate another Horner assertion that once individuals pledged to a candidate or cause, they become more susceptible to deceptive news reports that confirm their allegiance.

The two economists jointly surveyed a sample of Americans to measure the effects of fake news (some of which they made up themselves). A *New York Times* article describing the study summed up the findings: "People's hunger for information that suits their prejudices is powerful, and in the digital media age, a pile of it emerges to satisfy that demand." (www.nytimes.com/2017/01/18/upshot/researchers-created-fake-news-heres-what-they-found.html; Study: http://web.stanford.edu/~gentzkow/research/fakenews.pdf.)

Following the 2016 election, as critics began lambasting social media companies for allowing the circulation of fake-news attacks, both Google and Facebook announced plans to crack down on the sources. But a story in *Fortune* magazine questioned whether the problem was fixable, given First Amendment issues and a human tendency to share "what we want to believe." (http://fortune.com/2016/11/17/fake-news-problem.)

Looking Beyond Fake Political Stories

"Click bait" is a phrase now being used for news stories that are designed to get you to read them, even though they may be outrageous in their claims.

While some fake-news purveyors may have a political purpose, quite often the goal is simply to deliver you (and, by implication, your students) to their advertisers. We can see constant examples of what's called "native advertising" as we trawl websites each day – including some of the most prestigious news and information platforms. Click on a headline and you're suddenly reading a newsy-sounding story pitching a product – or you're staring at display ads tailored to your known interests (determined by tracking software on your device) – or both.

At the sites of CNN, the *New York Times*, and other more-trusted online sources, it's true that the headlines may appear in an area marked "Paid Content." But how discerning are students about these distinctions?

In a 2016 study, Stanford Graduate School of Education professor Sam Wineburg found that "82 percent of middle school students could not distinguish between a native ad sponsored content and a real news story." (http://sanfrancisco.cbslocal.com/2016/11/22/teens-vulnerable-to-fake-digital-news-stories.)

Activity: Sorting out Real News from Fake News

If I were addressing this problem in a 21st-century classroom, I think I would start by asking students: *what is news and who delivers it?* Can your students distinguish between purposeful, legitimate news and the other stuff out there? This seems a good place to start.

- Ask students to bring two examples to class – a story they believe is real news and a story they believe is fake. They may find them in newspapers and magazines or print them from the Internet. Make two piles and choose several examples (three might be good) from each category for class exploration. Research your choices in advance so you know the real facts about each.
- Mix the examples you've selected and project them one at a time, without indicating which pile they originated from. Have students, through polling or a show of hands, indicate "fake" or "real" for each example.
- Return to the first example and have students (as a whole or in small groups) consider the following critical thinking questions, drawn from the work of media literacy educators and organizations:
    - At a glance, does the headline or story seem believable or not so believable?
    - Who created the message? (author, producer)
    - Who is the message intended for? (audience, demographic)
    - What techniques does the producer use to make the message credible or believable?
    - What details might be omitted and why?
    - Where might we go to check the accuracy of this information?
- Students might then work in groups. Assign each group a story and have them use the Internet in an attempt to authenticate the story using the guiding questions. Or teachers (prepared in advance) might reveal facts about each story's credibility in a general discussion. The activity might end with reactions from students who selected the particular stories that were studied. Were they fooled?

Deciphering What's True or Not Is Harder than Ever

With social media's popularity as a news source, it's more important than ever that we equip students with the media literacy/critical thinking skills to distinguish fact from fiction. Admittedly, it's a challenging task. But our civil society depends on a well-informed citizenry – including tomorrow's voters.

Primary Resources

- I highly recommend that teachers explore this *New York Times* Learning Network article (January 19, 2017) sharing many lesson ideas and resources: "Evaluating Sources in a 'Post-Truth' World: Ideas for Teaching and Learning About Fake News." www.nytimes.com/2017/01/19/learning/lesson-plans/evaluating-sources-in-a-post-truth-world-ideas-for-teaching-and-learning-about-fake-news.html.
- *A Finder's Guide To Facts*, written by NPR's Steve Inskeep, provides a series of questions students can ask to determine if a news story is fake: http://n.pr/2gtmrP8.
- *How to Spot Fake News* offers a detailed discussion by the editors of the non-profit FactCheck.org: http://bit.ly/2tBi5uD.
- Organizations such as the Center for Media Literacy, The News Literacy Project, and the National Association of Media Literacy Education can provide guidance and more ideas about ways to evaluate truthfulness and accuracy, including lesson plans.
- Another helpful resource is the 2016 Stanford History Education Group study, *Evaluating Information: The Cornerstone of Civic Online Reasoning*, which includes examples of student tasks that were used to gauge the online reasoning capacity of nearly 8,000 diverse students: http://stanford.io/2gkkfXe.
- This account by a high school teacher describing his "fake news" lesson points out some of the nuances of approaching this topic: http://bit.ly/2sBUQMZ.

Media Link

The Stanford study has a helpful task in which students are asked to analyze the home page of Slate.com to determine what is news, what is an ad, etc. You can use it or create your own version with a different site. http://frankwbaker.com/mlc/stanford-fake-news-study.

Use Fact-Checking Websites

If you and your students doubt what you're reading is legitimate, there are now some excellent go-to websites that are reliable and trustworthy. These fact-checking websites are particularly useful in investigating politicians during speeches, interviews, and in social media and advertising:

- FactCheck.org is a project of the Annenberg Public Policy Center.
- The *Washington Post* Fact Checker examines statements and policy and politics for veracity and applies the Pinocchio Test to assign levels of accuracy: www.washingtonpost.com/news/fact-checker.
- Politifact.com from the *Tampa Bay Times* won a 2009 Pulitzer Prize for its work. It now supports state-level sites and a sister site PunditFact.com, which checks up on TV commentators. Both sites use the Truth-O-Meter to rate statements on a scale from True to "Pants on Fire" (Lie).
- Snopes.com has been fact-checking fake news, social media gossip, urban legends, and false claims since the early days of the public Internet (1995).

Additional Resources About "Native" Advertising

South Park Lampoon of Native Advertising Highlights Important Issues:

http://adage.com/article/digitalnext/south-park-lampoon-native-advertising-highlights-issues/302756

FTC Says Native Ads Must Carry Clear Disclosures:

www.mediapost.com/publications/article/265362/ftc-says-native-ads-must-carry-clear-disclosures.html

What Are the Implications of Ads that Know Our Search Histories?

http://theatln.tc/2tmUy10

November

Students are restless. They know there's a long Thanksgiving break coming up at the end of the month, then the run-up to Christmas. Meanwhile, it seems advertisers are pushing their winter holiday messages earlier and earlier in the calendar. After Halloween, the media is full of messages not only about Turkey Day but also the days immediately after that which will make or break many retailers' bottom line – Black Friday and Cyber Monday.

Black Friday ads, in fact, are a great way to engage students in an analysis of persuasive selling techniques. (Start a collection!) The first lesson in this chapter is about analyzing toy ads, one of the most potent and influential holiday sales messages. Toy ads are sure to grab the attention of tweens and young teens who still have an interest in fun and games.

The second lesson in this chapter takes a broader look at how students can go beyond seasonal ads and deconstruct marketing messages throughout their lives.

LESSON 10

Examining Holiday Toy Ads

Background

It's early fall as I write this, and already toy advertisers and marketers have their holiday ad plans in place. Their priority: the placement and positioning of their commercial spots on all of the networks that carry children's programs.

Despite the fascination with new media, children and their parents still watch television – lots of it. It's the job of the advertisers to know their demographic, and as technology advances and more and more social media data become available, it's easier than ever to target the toy-minded audience. You can be sure marketers know which TV shows kids of various ages (and their parents) watch most often.

As the holidays approach, using toy commercials in the classroom is a great way to jump-start media literacy. Media literacy, as I've defined it, is about *applying critical thinking/viewing skills to media messages*. And one of the most powerful media messages is the persuasive television commercial.

When most of us watch television, we've turned off the thinking parts of our brains. It's the job of educators to teach students how to turn on those "thinking parts" while we watch and develop critical thinking skills. And once kids begin to be discerning consumers of media, they can have a lot of fun deconstructing what they see.

Looking Behind the Scenes

Media literacy is also about understanding the production process, because most of us only see the finished media product – we rarely get to go behind the scenes to witness how a production moves from conception to completion. In my own teaching, I help young people comprehend and appreciate the tools (camera, lights, sound, special effects) and the techniques (camera angles, masculine/feminine colors, soft/loud music) used to make toy ads which appeal to their emotions.

Toy advertisers, like most other advertisers, know that they must showcase their products in the best possible light. Sometimes that means using tricks and hoping unsuspecting viewers won't notice. These finely crafted messages are some of the most persuasive and influential ads on television.

Here are two activities that I like to use in classrooms and teacher workshops. Each involves the marketing of two particular toys (as it happens, one that targets girls and one that targets boys). I've included a way to access the commercial for each of these products. They have a somewhat "old-timey" feel, but the sales techniques are pretty timeless, as you will see.

Activity 1: The Amazing Shrinking Vanity

Some years ago, one of the most popular toys of the holiday season was Cinderella's Magical Talking Vanity. I happened to be video recording one Saturday morning when a new ad for the product was broadcast during children's programming. In the 30-second commercial we see two young girls, both seated and standing next to the vanity. Here's my suggested plan:

1. Let students watch the commercial once. It's available on YouTube at www.youtube.com/watch?v=R9L_0cLejEA.
2. Ask them what questions they have about the toy, after a single viewing. Then, if need be, ask them a few questions of your own. You might wonder, for example: What makes the talking vanity "magical"? Why does the ad begin with a scene from Disney's Cinderella?
3. Show the commercial again. Before you do, ask students to be prepared to guess two things: the approximate age of the girls and the height of the vanity.
4. After they watch, you might use their answers about age to discuss the toy's "demographic." Why are the advertisers targeting this gender and age group? Would kids the age of your students be interested in such a toy? What TV shows might be the best places to advertise to this audience?
5. Record students' guesses about the vanity's height on your board. (The actual dimensions are 7.7" deep, 20" wide and 25.8" tall.) Take a yardstick or tape measure and show students 26 inches (the height) and ask them if they are surprised.
6. Then ask: Is this ad deceptive? Why or why not? If it is deceptive, is this kind of advertising fair?
7. If time allows, you might show the commercial a third time and ask students to watch for ways it makes the toy look more appealing. (Think about the setting, the music, the special effects, the girls' clothing, etc.)

At my website you'll find an actual photo of the toy (or search Google Images) and the actual description from Amazon: http://frankwbaker.com/mlc/toy-ads-cinderella-notes.

Activity 2: "Buy Me That!"

In 1990, HBO, in a collaboration with Consumer Reports Television, aired the first of three half-hour specials about children and advertising. The "Buy Me That!" programs helped pull back the curtain on many of the techniques and tricks used in TV commercials. These 30-minute shows – now unfortunately out of circulation – became favorites with media educators, myself included. (But read on and learn how to access a three-minute segment that's great for teaching.)

In one of the more popular segments, the producers showcase a remote-controlled toy boat branded the "Typhoon 2." In the commercial, the announcer proclaims loudly that it "zooms around that rocky maze" and "glides over water on a cushion of air." After running the ad, the Buy Me That producers show kids actually using the toy. They capture many of their very disappointed comments – also revealing that the toy costs $120 (that's 1990s dollars) and runs for only 10 minutes on a battery charge.

Fortunately, I have been able to obtain the Typhoon 2 segment (about three minutes). It's available on YouTube at www.youtube.com/v/2Hdm69hpO-E. This fascinating segment can be used in many ways, but here's a suggestion I have:

1. Show the segment without any backgrounding other than perhaps an explanation that it's for a 1990s toy. I like to stop the video just after the voiceover says "see how the Typhoon 2 zooms around that rocky maze." I ask students, "raise your hand if you'd like to have this toy." Most hands shoot up!
2. Finish watching the segment (perhaps show it a second time). Consider using some of these questions for discussion:

   - Who is this toy ad aimed at? What age group? What gender? Are most toy ads aimed at both boys and girls, or just one group or the other?
   - Would you agree with the show's host that this ad is deceptive? Why?
   - If you bought this toy after seeing the ad and had the experience the kids in the show had, who could you complain to? (When I have students brainstorm this question, typical answers include the President of the United States, the toy store, the toy company. It's rare that anyone suggests complaining to the TV network or station that aired the commercial. Then I'll ask, "don't broadcasters have an obligation to run advertising that is truthful and not deceptive?")

3. Ask students if they've ever had a similar experience – buying a toy based on advertising promises and then feeling deceived. Let them share some stories.
4. Ask them if they can think of a current toy ad that might be deceptive. Students could "investigate" via a homework assignment that has them

watching some children's commercial programming to spot possibilities and decide on which ad seems the most deceptive.
5. The next step will depend on your school situation, but my suggestion would be to (a) attempt to capture the ad or find it on YouTube or at the manufacturer's website, and (b) purchase or have a store donate the toy for student testing. At this point there are many learning opportunities: they could write up their findings (or use phones or a small camera to make a video review). They could write to the Federal Trade Commission, the broadcaster, the retailer, or the manufacturer. They could post their findings on your class website and share on social media.

It's Up to Us

Many toy commercials, then and now, have some element of deception. But many viewers (and most young people) are largely unaware. They've not been taught how to watch with a critical eye and see through the spin. This is where media literacy comes in.

Students who are not media literate will fall into the trap of believing everything they see, read, and hear. Today's teachers tell me that most of their students don't question: *If something is on TV (or the Internet), they believe it.* It's our job to use the media, and popular culture, as the hooks to teach critical thinking and educate savvy consumers.

On page 60 of this book is a Toy Ad Analysis Worksheet that you can adapt to both print and video analyzing. It is also available to download here: www.frankwbaker.com/toyadanalysisworksheet.htm.

Additional Resources

How Toy Advertising Influences Kids:

www.frankwbaker.com/toys

What Toy Commercials Are Really Selling (http://bit.ly/2uePA3K) by Michele Yulo. "Toy ads would have us believe that all girls are happy and love sunshine and cupcakes, while boys are active and busy building and smashing things."

Guys and Dolls: Why Kids' Advertising is Going Gender Neutral (http://bit.ly/2tfR79M), by Sarah Shearman.

The Gendering of Our Kids' Toys And What We Can Do About It (http://bit.ly/1SGmunk), by Elizabeth Sweet.

TV Toy Ad Analysis Worksheet

created by Frank Baker ©2005

Teachers: use this worksheet as a handout for students who will be studying television toy advertising. As students watch commercials, they should fill in the blanks below. For more info go to www.frankwbaker.com/toys.htm

Name of toy/ Manufacturer	*Techniques of persuasion	Target age/ Gender	Age of kids in ad	Small print	Actor expressions	Memorable phrases or slogans	Visuals (lights, color, special effects)	Sound (including music)

***Common techniques of persuasion:** Source: www.agclassroom.org/teacher/pdf/key_ingredients.pdf

Cool kids: everybody wants to be these kids

Family fun: the ad shows a product as something that instantly helps families have fun together

Excitement: the product is the key to amazing fun and adventure

Star power: a huge celebrity uses this product

Bigger is better: this ad makes the product look bigger than it actually is

Repetition: manufacturers hope that if you see or hear the product name a lot, you will want it

Feel good: this ad tells a story that makes you feel good

Sounds good: manufacturers use music and other sound effects to grab your attention and make the product appealing

What's missing?: the ad doesn't give you the full story about the product

Cartoon characters: they help you remember the product (example: Tony the Tiger)

Weasely words: using words or phrases that are misleading

Looking Beyond the Toy Ads to a World Saturated with Marketing Messages

Background

We've had students examine toy advertising in Lesson 10. And toys are a good hook into the topic. But toy ads are just a small part of the picture. In today's culture, we are under bombardment. We rarely if ever find ourselves in an environment completely free of ads and other marketing materials. So the "Black Friday" season seems a good time to also look at advertising more generally.

As media literacy educators work to engage students in conversations and study about commercial marketing, we have to encompass more advertising in more mediums (radio, TV, film, Internet, newspapers, magazines, social media) than ever before.

Common Core Connections

In the pre-Common Core era, we were teaching students "techniques of persuasion." Now, as we've discussed, the terminology has shifted to "argument." The study of advertising fits nicely in many Common Core standards, including these two:

Speaking and Listening Standards (Grade 8): Analyze the purpose of information presented in diverse media and formats (e.g., visually, quantitatively, orally) and evaluate the motives (e.g., social, commercial, political) behind its presentation.

College and Career Readiness Anchor Standards for Reading (Integration): Delineate and evaluate the argument and specific claims in a text, including the validity of the reasoning as well as the relevance and sufficiency of the evidence.

Deconstructing Ads Throughout the School Year

Sometimes you'll want to do thematic lessons on ads, such as during holiday toy season or during the Super Bowl season (see Lesson 14). However, you can look at advertisements and marketing messages any time of the year. For example, look at food commercials, makeup ads, car commercials, technology ads, and more.

Remember, the media literacy approach recommends that we challenge our students to think about:

- how an ad was constructed;
- for what audience(s);
- using which techniques; and
- who benefits from the message and its placement.

An art approach might involve studying layout, design, color, font, and image composition.

For English language arts and social studies teachers: Think about the words "purpose" and "motive" in the Common Core 8th-grade standard. Ask students "what is the purpose of advertising?" and most will probably say to sell something. But I would argue that advertising is much more than simply selling.

More than anything, it's about persuasion. Challenge students to create a log of all the ads they come into contact with during a typical day. Where did they see the ads? What do they recall? Are they influenced by ads? (Just ask them to explain the logos on their clothes.)

Activity 1: Deconstructing a Pizza Ad

1. Show students an advertisement for pizza. The Media Link box below will send you to an ad taken from a magazine aimed at the tween audience.

Media Link

A pizza ad students can analyze: http://frankwbaker.com/pizza_ad.

I introduce this ad by recommending that my audience:

- read every word on the page (even words in small font);
- make a list of all of the images;
- consider the layout, color, design, and font.

I advise students to raise their hands if they come across any unfamiliar words.

Speaking of words, did you notice those words in small font running along the left margin of the ad? They might be something important, and I like to get my audience to rotate the ad horizontally to read those small words.

2. So how else might we use this ad? We might ask students to identify the slogan; tell the story; notice the colors and other attention-getters; identify the point of view; who has the power; how does your eye move as you read the ad?
3. We can take the ad deconstruction even further by challenging students to consider these questions:
   - who created this ad? (the answer is not on the ad)
   - what is the purpose of the ad?
   - who is the audience for the ad; what are the clues?
   - what magazine would you expect to publish an ad like this?
   - what is omitted and why? and where can students find the answers to what's missing?

(Here is the full lesson plan, www.frankwbaker.com/sde_lesson_plan_template_2, I used for a South Carolina project, with this pizza ad. You can find all the background information about the ad you need. There's also an 8.5 × 11 download – large enough to read all the small print.)

After your students have gained experience in analyzing ads, you should consider giving them opportunities to create ads. (Creation sits atop the list of higher-order thinking skills in this proposed Bloom's Digital Taxonomy: http://edorigami.wikispaces.com/Bloom's+Digital+Taxonomy.)

Activity 2: Using VoiceThread

Several years ago, I discovered a middle-grades teacher who was using VoiceThread to engage her students in ad analysis and deconstruction. Take a look and listen (http://ed.voicethread.com/share/663006) to how her students responded to the NIKE ad and the questions she posed.

Try VoiceThread or a similar tool to help your own students analyze ads.

Activity 3: Writing Ad Scripts

Do your students know that commercials are first written before they are produced? One strategy might be to introduce the simple one-page commercial script format. My "Scriptwriting in the Classroom" website (www.frankwbaker.com/scriptwriting_in_the_classroom) offers many resources in this regard, including sample ad scripts (www.frankwbaker.com/scriptwriting_tv.htm).

Before showing students commercials, you might begin by having them write their own commercials or PSA (Public Service Announcements). A simple two-column script has AUDIO and VIDEO. If students try their hand at writing a commercial, since they're not shooting the video they should concentrate on AUDIO (what is being said and heard). Audio includes not only the narration (on camera or voiceover), but also the music and sound effects.

Scriptwriting alone is a valuable Common Core-related activity, and it can be made more valuable by also having your students "storyboard" (draw) the action that the script describes. (I spotted several introductory storyboard videos on TeacherTube.com.)

Should you decide to let students work on video, remember that it is both the script and the storyboard that must precede production. So before your students turn on those cameras, make sure they've completed the first two steps.

Script + Storyboard = Production

Activity 4: Deconstructing a TV Commercial

This YouTube page shows a commercial for cell phones: www.youtube.com/watch?v=rb9XVKSb1XU. For years, ever since I first saw this commercial, I have been using it in my media literacy workshops. We know that young people watch a lot of TV, and so we know they are exposed to a lot of commercials, even though they may zap (skip) them.

Most of our young people already own mobile (cell) phones – they're already connected. But if we ask these same young people – how was the cell phone first marketed? – this question alone is a good backgrounder for what they are about to see.

Teaching advertising is a great way to infuse media literacy, critical viewing, and higher-order thinking skills into instruction. We know our students are targets for all kinds of products and services. We know that advertisers use every trick in the book (techniques of persuasion) to make their products attractive, appealing, and believable. We also know that most students watch media passively. Media literacy, among other things, is designed to turn them into active (questioning) thinkers/viewers.

For the most part, students have never been taught how to watch or deconstruct television. (For that matter, many educators have never had a minute of media literacy training.) This activity involves listening to and viewing a commercial for cell phones. Students will be encouraged to look deeply and to ask questions about the production techniques used to make the commercial. (Most national and state standards for English language arts include both "viewing" and "listening," so this activity can help educators fulfill those objectives.)

1. Previewing questions. Students should be challenged with questions like:
    - who creates commercials and for what purpose?
    - what techniques do the creators use to make a product appealing?
    - how do they know who might be their "target audience"?
    - which specific "techniques of persuasion" might be used in this ad?
    - which television shows will the creators buy time within to show the ad?
    - how much does it cost to make an ad; to position it inside a prime-time program?
    - how are camerawork, lighting, music, and editing used to tell the story?
    - how do I feel after seeing a commercial? How does it appeal to my emotions?
2. Now get started by asking your students to simply close their eyes while you play back the one-minute ad.
3. At the end of the minute, ask them to open their eyes and to write down everything they heard. Now, why is this important? Most of us are visual learners. Yet commercials are composed of both visuals *and* sounds. (A simple two-column script is how most commercials are formatted; see worksheet on page 66.) This exercise is designed to get them to think about the audio (sound) portion of what they experience. Give your students about a minute to make their list. After the minute, you should ask: what did you hear? Be prepared to write their responses on the board, overhead, or WhiteBoard. Invariably, some students may have heard things in the commercial that others in the class did not hear. For example, ask how many heard the wolf (or dog) howling. For those who did not hear it, you can point this out in the next step.
4. Be prepared to play the commercial a second time, this time allowing them to see it for the first time. Before doing so, ask your students this question: Other than cell phones, what else is being sold? (This question is designed to get them thinking about how the creator of the cell phone ad used techniques to sell . . . fear, for example.) After the second viewing, ask students the question: what else is being sold? (Did they answer fear?) Why would cell phone makers use fear to sell their products? What techniques did they use to "sell" fear? (Students should think about specific words, phrases, sounds, music, etc.) Can they think of any people who have used fear to sell products/concepts/issues/candidates?

Worksheet, Two-Column Script

Video	Audio

5. Post-viewing questions: Introduce students to the "languages of television/video production" – these are the tools producers use not only to create media, but also to create meaning. Introduce these before proceeding to the next step.

   Cameras:

   1. Camera shots (where is the camera positioned? close-up, far away)
   2. Camera lens (does the lens zoom in or out?)
   3. Camera movement (does the camera tilt, pan, truck?)

   Lighting: what time of day is depicted? What clues tell you so?

   Music: what types of instruments do you hear?

   Sounds: other than music, what other sounds are heard (e.g. female narrator, car cranking, sound of cars going by; dog (wolf) howl, etc.)

   Setting: where is the location? Is it artificial or real? Justify your response.

   Post production: editing; what impact does it have?

   Actors' expression: other than words, notice how an actor communicates with facial expression, body language, gestures.

6. Play the commercial again. If you have time, play the commercial a third time: assign groups of students to one of the languages of television/video production. They will be responsible for discussing the ad from their groups' assignment.

Possible questions:

- how many close-ups, medium shots, wide shots?
- why is lighting important? How does it help to set the mood?
- describe the music; does it remind you of something?
- how do sound effects contribute to the feel of this spot?
- what is the setting; how do you know; is it realistic?
- count the number of edits (the number of times the shot changes). Students should count out loud.

After this screening, you might ask: what is the impact of quick edits?

- what non-verbal expressions are used that might reveal how she is feeling, thinking?
- what happens at the end of the commercial? Why do you think the producer of the commercial stopped it like that? What do you think might happen next?
- power: who has power and who is powerless in the ad? How does that make you feel?

7. Optional: Have students create the actual script for this commercial. See the blank script template shown earlier in this activity (on page 66 in this book) Ask students to re-create the script. In the video column they should make a list of each shot and describe it in detail. In the audio column, they should document everything that is heard.

Teaching tip: You could do this lesson with other commercials as well. Choose a commercial spot that you think will resonate with your students. For younger students, I recommend a toy commercial; for older students it might be one for fast food, diet products, or a candidate running for office. Plan to show the spot more than once: that way, students will pick up elements they may have missed on first viewing. One element that you can particularly call students' attention to is production techniques. How might understanding camerawork, lighting, sound, editing, etc. help students understand how these elements imply meaning?

Additional Resources

If you have students create PSAs instead of commercials, you might find these sites useful:

The PSA Research Center contains examples and guidelines: www.psaresearch.com.

Examples of PSAs can be found here: http://saloproductions.com/public-service-announcements/psa-samples

December

The month of December finds many of us thinking about the end of another calendar year and the upcoming holidays.

We are all bombarded by advertising and marketing messages because it is that time of year.

Critical viewing and media literacy require that we understand and question these messages.

Some of these messages use humor as the technique of persuasion. Therefore, the first lesson in this chapter has students analyze parody.

Critical viewing also requires that we understand how Big Media companies work. The second lesson in this chapter helps students be aware of these corporate giants controlling much of the country's media.

LESSON 12

Engaging in the Study of Parody

Background

Let's agree: it's not just middle school students who love parody – many of us do.

Whether it's *MAD* magazine, *The Simpsons*, *The Onion*, *Saturday Night Live*, or some recently altered image on the web, parody seems to be not only popular but also everywhere. Students might be most familiar with it through memes on Instagram and other social media sites.

Parody is defined as imitation, sometimes exaggerated for comic effect.

So parody is poking fun at something in hopes the audience will find it amusing. But first, the audience must make the connection between the parody and the subject/topic being parodied.

In the Common Core State Standards for English language arts, parody is listed as one of the genres educators should use with students (see Standard 10: Range, Quality and Complexity for grades 6–12).

One of my earliest media literacy experiences with parody came when I was developing an activity centered around analyzing magazine ads for cigarettes. (As in most media literacy activities, students should be engaged in both analyzing and creating some form of media.) While I had plenty of ads from magazines for students to deconstruct, I had not yet developed an activity around creating, until I saw my first tobacco ad parody. (Since then, there have been hundreds of parody ads created: www.google.com/search?q=parody+tobacco+ads&biw=1140&bih=527&tbm=isch&tbo=u&source=univ&sa=X&ved=0ahUKEwjmzZHMw__LAhVE4iYKHSBBBqcQsAQIIg.)

On my website is an example featuring an original ad for KOOL cigarettes and then a parody that alters one letter in the brand name, completely changing the meaning (see Media Link box).

Media Link

Access the KOOL ad and parody here: www.frankwbaker.com/koolfool.htm.

So, after showing students plenty of other counter-advertising parodies, I challenged them to create their own tobacco ads based on ones they were assigned to study. They were advised to consider altering the words, images, and even the Surgeon General's warning in the box.

On my website is a student example (see Media Link). The student-created ad was recognized in Washington State and made part of a state-wide anti-tobacco movement aimed at young people.

Media Link

Camel counter ad: www.frankwbaker.com/camelcounterad.htm.

Not only can these ads be humorous, they can also be effective at challenging the tobacco industry's huge promotional and advertising campaigns.

In this parody movie trailer, Secrets of a Tobacco Executive (https://vimeo.com/39604742), viewers might be fooled into believing that this is a real movie, because it begins with the MPAA ratings slide, followed by the logo of an official-looking studio sponsor, and dramatic male voiceover. (Ask your students if this is a movie they'd like to see.)

Parody in the Race for the White House

MAD magazine has to be the leader in parody, since it was first published in the early 1950s. No subject is off-limits to *MAD* writers and illustrators. During the last election, *MAD* took aim at Republican candidate Donald Trump and Democratic candidate Hillary Clinton. (Would your students understand what Oscar-winning film the Clinton cover references?)

Media Link

See the political *MAD* covers here: http://frankwbaker.com/mlc/mad-magazine-covers.

While print is a popular medium for parody, non-print is not immune.

Two organizations have produced parody presidential campaign commercials. The first, for "candidate" Gil Fulbright, is noteworthy because it pulls back the curtain on many of the production techniques used by real candidates. "A dramatic camera angle," says the candidate in a voiceover, "can make me look like a president."

Honest Gil (as he calls himself) says he has the "courage to point" – poking fun at what other politicians seem to do in their ads. He also calls attention to the fact that most candidates spend most of their time raising huge sums of money, which is true. Take a look at his ad here: www.youtube.com/watch?v=NAtunJv6NtE.

Another parody ad promotes itself as using "stock images." (Stock images are not photos that are created for the purpose of the ad, but rather those that are previously captured and purchased from a company.) Buzzfeed found several examples of stock images being used in the 2012 race for the White House.

In another example, Dissolve has created the Generic Presidential Campaign Ad, featuring the smiling candidate standing in front of an American flag and the slogan: "Candidate for American America" (whatever that means).

The candidate with no name says, among other things, "My record shows that I can construct a narrative by keeping the details pretty vague," again poking fun at what actual candidates say, or don't say, in their advertising.

Media Link

Buzzfeed stock examples: www.buzzfeed.com/andrewkaczynski/13-presidential-campaign-ad-stock-images-and-the-o#.dmG7OoEzE.

Dissolve Generic Presidential Ad example: www.youtube.com/watch?v=rouDlzhgVcY.

Activity: Teaching With and About Parody

So why not engage your students in parody and the various mediums in which it can be found? Here's one way to approach this:

1. Assign your students a medium. This can be radio, TV, magazines, newspapers, motion pictures, etc.
2. Have them first research how parody has been used in their medium.
3. Have your students study the techniques that make parody particularly effective to that medium.
4. Next, assign them a book, news article, movie, magazine cover, or song. Working in groups, they have to create a parody from their original media. Their creation can be either print or non-print.

Yes, parody can be fun and engaging. It can also be effective at helping students recognize techniques used in making these unique messages. If you have your students create their own parodies, you're also helping meet those 21st-century media literacy skills which include analyzing and creating media messages.

Additional Resources

Frank Baker's Parody Website:

http://frankwbaker.com/mlc/parody-satire

ReadWriteThink.org (search for parody lesson plans and ideas).

Web English Teacher:

www.webenglishteacher.com/parodies.html

The Simpsons Parodies Presidential Debates:

http://screenrant.com/the-simpsons-2016-presidential-debates-clip.

Weird Al Yankovic Best Parodies:

www.azcentral.com/story/entertainment/music/2014/07/16/weird-al-yankovic-best-songs-parodies/12743759

How Big Media Influences the News We Read

Background

In 1983, majority control of U.S. media organizations was held by 50 corporations. After 35 years of mergers and acquisitions, that number has been reduced from 50 to five or six, often referred to as "Big Media."

Although the definition of a "media organization" is difficult to nail down, we might think of them as organizations that curate and manage the flow of news and information to the general public. One definition used by the federal courts reads:

> a person or entity engaged in disseminating information to the general public through a newspaper, magazine, other publication, radio, television, cable television, or other medium of mass communication.
> (2 USCS § 1602)

A more practical way to define today's media organizations might be to look at a list. According to *Forbes* magazine, "The World's Largest Media Companies of 2015" included (in the U.S.) Comcast, Walt Disney, 21st Century Fox, Time Warner, Time Warner Cable (now owned by Charter), DirecTV (now part of AT&T), CBS, and Viacom.

Students might not think of cable companies like Comcast or entertainment companies like Disney as "news and information" entities. Yet over the past four decades these mega-corporations have absorbed most of the organizations that Americans rely upon to understand what's going on in the world.

Comcast, for example, owns NBC and Telemundo and many cable-only channels including MSNBC, CNBC, USA Network, NBCSN, E!, and The Weather Channel. Disney's empire includes ABC, ABC News, and ESPN, in addition to its film and entertainment companies. Time Warner, which may be acquired by AT&T in 2017, controls CNN and its global network of news channels. 21st Century Fox owns Fox News and Fox Sports – and its sister company NewsCorp owns the *Wall Street Journal*, the *New York Post*, and hundreds of newspapers and magazines worldwide.

Understanding these kinds of connections, at least in a broad sense, is an important part of being media-literate in the 21st century. Even more important, perhaps, is that students understand how these mega-corporations are able to use their array of news, entertainment, and information delivery systems to cross-market products and programs – often while giving the appearance of being "unconnected."

What are the ramifications/implications if only a half-dozen companies control a majority of American media? One response is that there are fewer voices out there; it becomes harder to get a diversity of opinion. Another might be that the most *important* news increasingly gives way to the most *profitable* news.

In terms of prior knowledge, students need to understand the basic history of broadcasting rights and the original pact between broadcasting license owners and the American people – free exclusive use of communication bands in return for objective reporting in the public interest.

The Walt Disney Company provides a good example for discussion. Most of us are familiar with Walt Disney's theme parks in Florida and California. Disney also produces lots of television programs and movies. Students will know of one of their recent films, *Star Wars: The Force Awakens*, which became the highest-grossing film of all time in early 2016. But do students know what else Disney controls?

In late 2015 *Wired* magazine published an infographic showing Disney's current holdings. It's available online at: www.wired.com/2015/11/how-disney-is-making-sure-youll-never-be-able-to-escape-star-wars.

With everything that Disney owns (ABC, ESPN, Lucasfilm, A&E, Hulu, and more), it's not hard to understand how it can successfully promote a product (a personality, toy, movie, TV show, concert) through any or all of its holdings. By conveying a specific message through its networks – including news outlets once considered "objective" – Disney can insure that many of us will know whatever they want us to know.

Why does "Good Morning America" on the ABC TV Network sometimes broadcast "live" from Disney World, instead of its usual studio in Times Square, New York City? Why would "World News Tonight," ABC's primary evening newscast, air a feature on Star Wars or the latest Disney animated feature? It's all about financial synergy.

As Big Media companies acquire more properties and influence in cities and local communities, this synergy extends into local television, radio, and cable information systems. One way for students to "think global" is to "analyze local" – in this case, learning more about the media ownership in their own communities.

Activity: Big Media Comes to Town

1. Begin with some exploration and discussion of the Big Media trend. The background provided above and the resources listed below can spark ideas for this lesson. Teachers might, for example, watch the Bill Moyers segment "Big Money, Big Media, Big Trouble" and look for excerpts related to "Big Media" that are suitable for student viewing (http://billmoyers.com/episode/big-money-big-media-big-trouble).

I also recommend reading a perspective article published by Truthout in March 2016 (also available at Moyers' site), "Twenty Years of Media Consolidation Has Not Been Good for Our Democracy," to gain perspective on the politics behind the growth of Big Media (http://billmoyers.com/story/twenty-years-of-media-consolidation-has-not-been-good-for-our-democracy).

2. Ask your students to investigate who owns the media in your community. Consider radio stations, newspapers, TV stations, cable companies, Internet-based news, billboard companies, etc. Is there a pattern? Does one company own more than one radio station in your community; is that problematic? (Older students might review the evolution of FCC ownership rules: www.fcc.gov/consumers/guides/fccs-review-broadcast-ownership-rules.)

Do the media in your community cover local issues and events adequately? Does it matter whether the news is owned/produced by someone local or a national corporation?

A good example of what can happen when distant media own local media outlets occurred in North Dakota. The 2002 event, an overnight toxic chemical train derailment, and the subsequent inability to get word to local residents, is documented in the book *Fight for Air: The Battle to Control America's Media* (2007) by Eric Klinenberg. The *Washington Post* summarized the story:

> When a train derailment in the middle of the night released a frightening cloud of anhydrous ammonia, Minot police sought to notify the citizenry of the crisis. They called KCJB, the (radio) station designated as the local emergency broadcaster, but no one was home; the station was being run by computer, automatically passing along Clear Channel programming from another city.
>
> (www.slate.com/articles/news_and_politics/press_box/2007/01/what_really_happened_in_minot_nd.html)

Additional Resources

Industry Publications

Multichannel News

Broadcasting & Cable Magazine

Recent example: "Redstones Call Off CBS-Viacom Merger" (December 12, 2016)

Public Interest Organizations Focused on Media Responsibility

Norman Lear Center studies "the impact of entertainment and media on society":

https://learcenter.org

Media Impact Project:

www.mediaimpactproject.org

Bill Moyers.com (Public Square Media):

http://billmoyers.com

The Poynter Institute:

www.poynter.org

Media Research and Analysis

"How Americans Get Their News" (2016), Pew Research Center:

www.journalism.org/2016/07/07/pathways-to-news.

"Comcast, AT&T, and ISP lobbyists are excited about Trump's FCC chair" – Ars Technica (January 2017):

https://arstechnica.co.uk/tech-policy/2017/01/comcast-att-and-isp-lobbyists-are-excited-about-trumps-fcc-chair.

Media Ownership and Democracy in the Digital Information Age: Promoting Diversity with First Amendment Principles and Market Structure Analysis (Center for Internet & Society, Stanford Law School – a book exploring policy ideas to reduce Big Media influence):

https://cyberlaw.stanford.edu/attachments/mediabooke.pdf.

A Final Note: Stay Alert

Media ownership is constantly combining and morphing, so teachers and students need to be alert to the accuracy of any statements about who owns what at any given time.

One notable example: Internet pioneer AOL was organized in the 1990s, eventually became powerful enough to buy Time Warner in 2000, but failed to thrive and eventually was spun off by Time Warner in 2009. Over the next six years AOL strengthened with deals like the purchase of *Huffington Post* and partnerships with top ad-selling rivals like Yahoo and Microsoft. In 2015, AOL was purchased by Verizon. AOL chief Tim Armstrong said at the time: "If you look forward five years, you're going to be in a space where there are going to be massive, global-scale networks, and there's no better partner for us." "For now," he might have added.

What continues to be clear is that giant media, Internet, and communications companies understand the power and profit associated with owning news and information properties that exert huge influence over consumer spending. This is the essential lesson to be learned by us and our students.

Credit: Some of this material comes from my book, *Media Literacy in the K-12 Classroom*, 2nd Edition (ISTE, 2016).

January

The news this New Year will be filled with ads about going on a diet (after the holidays) and the upcoming Super Bowl football game. The diet industry depends on the media to get their messages to millions of overweight consumers. Meanwhile, other advertisers will pay huge sums of money just to get their messages in front of millions of people. Do you or your students recall any product or message from last year's game? Why do advertisers spend millions of dollars on ONE 30-second ad? Getting your students interested in Super Bowl advertising is another one of those teachable moment opportunities.

Another teachable opportunity is in January and into February when we recognize Dr. Martin Luther King, Jr. and during Black History month when we encourage students to study accomplishments of famous and not-so-famous African Americans.

LESSON 14

Looking Deeper into Super Bowl Ads

Background

As I noted earlier, for many years, I have hosted a web page, "Using Super Bowl Ads in the Classroom" (www.frankwbaker.com/mlc/super-bowl-ads). I wanted to help educators who haven't thought about using these popular culture texts in instruction. You might notice that I use the word "texts." TV and other video commercials should be considered as texts because they present information that students can learn to scrutinize closely (analyze) and deconstruct. In fact, the National Council of Teachers of English has long recommended that teachers include "non-print" texts in the classroom.

In a study I conducted some years ago, elements of media literacy were found in the English language arts (ELA) teaching standards of most states. Understanding advertising continues to be an important part of media literacy today. The Common Core ELA standards also speak to the need to engage students in these real-world, popular culture "informational texts."

Standards aside, can there be any doubt that students today are bombarded by commercial messages everywhere they look on every device they use, and need to be smart and discerning about what they see and hear?

In my media literacy workshops around the nation, I often hear from teachers who are still not comfortable teaching with or about advertising. One reason is a lack of training or the need to simply think all the way through the process. If you find yourself in this category, read on.

The Super Bowl Ad Extravaganza

First, let's look at some background on the Super Bowl ad extravaganza. In 2016, the Super Bowl game was viewed by 100+ million people in the U.S. alone (NBC had an average audience of 114.4 million viewers in 2015) and the cost of a 30-second ad was estimated at $5 million this time around (up 10%). At this stage of the run-up to the game, a lot of attention (on social media, in the press, and around the office water cooler) had already been given to the game and the commercials (each year, look no further than USA Today's AdMeter site: http://admeter.usatoday.com).

One marketing professor, writing at the *Huffington Post* (www.huffington post.com/ira-kalb/super-bowl-ads-provide-a_b_9034060.html), noted (critically) that advertisers would likely spend another $1 million or more in 2017 to produce their commercial, pushing the cost up to $6 million or $200,000 a second. How can these expensive, high-concept advertisements, which will appear over the course of a seven-hour broadcast, be used in the classroom?

The producers and creators of commercials use a formula they know will hook the audience. It might be humor, a slogan, a jingle, a color, a pet, a celebrity . . . anything they believe (and market testing shows) will attract positive attention to their product.

It's up to us, as educators, to pull back the curtain on how these highly persuasive texts might pull an emotional string which makes us remember (or want to purchase) the product or spread the message.

Students Need to Think like Advertisers

When I speak to teachers about advertising, I encourage them to get their students to think as if THEY were advertisers. If you are going to promote a product, then you must know:

- who is my audience?
- what are the best ways to reach them?
- what techniques will I use to get and hold their attention?
- what celebrity or high-profile event can I associate with?
- what television programs and websites does my audience follow closely?
- what do I want them to know about my product?
- how can I get them to make a purchase?

Years ago, I developed a series of media literacy/critical thinking questions and posted them on my Super Bowl ads web page (www.frankwbaker.com/mlc/super-bowl-ads). You'll find several current links there, including this story about a non-profit in New York that lets youth remix Super Bowl ads (www.thelampnyc.org/2014/01/22/press-release-nyc-nonprofit-the-lamp-holds-event-for-youth-to-remix-super-bowl-commercials-in-real-time/?utm_source=twitterfeed&utm_medium=twitter&utm_campaign=Feed:+TheLamp+%28The+LAMP%29) in real time. And there's even SuperBowl-Ads.com, a website that includes information about the commercials featured during the professional football championship game in past years, as well as news about the 2015 and 2016 commercials (teacher discretion advised).

Activity 1: Questions to Consider Before the Kickoff

Here are some questions you might have students research and ponder *before* the game:

- What do you know about the Super Bowl game? Where did you learn it? Why does the game get tremendous media attention every year? What makes advertisers want to show their ads during this once-a-year sporting event? Why does it cost so much to buy just one 30-second ad? What justifies that advertising expense? How do advertisers make money from their Super Bowl spots?
- Students might also use search tools to find out who decides in what order the ads air during the game. Why do some ads only run in certain sections of the United States? How do advertisers create buzz about their ads, even before the game is broadcast? They might create a chart listing the known advertisers (http://adage.com/article/special-report-super-bowl/super-bowl-xlix-ad-chart-buying-big-game-commercials/295841) and research their parent companies.
- They might predict how many ads will be for: alcohol? cars? TV shows? movies? Why are some kinds of ads so popular with Super Bowl advertisers (e.g., beer, wine, liquor)?
- Which propaganda/persuasion techniques (www.slideshare.net/jadajadajingjing/persuasion-techniques-22556467) would you expect to be used in each ad? Which ad(s) are you looking forward to viewing and why?

(Here is one teacher's Super Bowl assignment for students: www.oconee.k12.sc.us/webpages/ccarlisle/index.cfm?subpage=46382.)

Be on the lookout for not-so-obvious ads during the broadcast – like the Pepsi half-time moments. (Students might want to create a list.) Based on the ads scheduled to be broadcast, what demographic (gender, age) do you think each advertiser is trying to reach? What social media might be used, if at all, by advertisers during the event window? How do students plan to use social media, if at all, during the game?

(USA Today, online and in the print edition, includes AdMeter (http://admeter.usatoday.com), a huge preview of the ads in the Friday issue before the game.)

Activity 2: Questions to Consider After the Game

Here are some questions to consider *after* the game (in addition to "Who won and what was the score?"):

- What ad(s) did you find most entertaining, and why? (Students should be specific and give details here.) What ad(s) did you find the most dull/lame, and why? Which ad(s) did you think were most effective in getting viewers to buy or do something, and why? Which ads were for products or services that you couldn't figure out?
- Which ad(s) were you most willing to share (email, likes, retweets) with friends? Which ad(s) featured well-known personalities? Why? Which "techniques of persuasion" were used in each ad? Teachers might want to select appropriate elements from this media investigations checklist (http://web.archive.org/web/20071105204037/http:/reta.nmsu.edu/traincd/media/tools.html) and have students match the ads with techniques described on the list.
- Math? Students might calculate the total advertising revenue going to the TV network if each 30-second ad costs an estimated $5 million. Older students can do more sophisticated calculations (www.yummymath.com/2015/super-bowl-ads-2015). (*An aside:* Ads are cheaper if they are targeted at smaller audiences; e.g., the 2015 Verge ad that appeared in only one Montana city and cost $700.)
- How do Super Bowl advertisers get mileage for their message before and after the game? How many ads did you spot inside the stadium? How were Twitter, Facebook, Instagram, and other social media used during the game to promote the products being advertised? How did you use them, if at all?
- Students might survey classmates, parents, and grandparents and ask each to list their three favorite ads. Compare and contrast responses. Do some ads appeal to different genders and age groups? Were these the groups the ads were targeting?
- GoDaddy and Budweiser had competing "cute puppy" ads in 2015. GoDaddy's ad had to be withdrawn. The ad distressed social media users when they learned that the ad's narrative ended with Buddy the puppy being listed for sale online as soon as he found his lost family. Know your audience? GoDaddy's announcement included an apology, and in an earlier tweet, CEO Blake Irving said it was intended to be a "fun and funny ad." These developments might make for a good class discussion. "Why did GoDaddy's attempt at fun backfire?" Find a scene-by-scene look at the heart-warming Budweiser ad in this video: http://larryferlazzo.edublogs.org/2016/02/07/video-close-reading-a-super-bowl-commercial, from Poynter.

Taking the time to use Super Bowl advertising in your classroom and having students discuss their opinions is another great way of demonstrating that popular culture and media literacy have a place in today's 21st-century classrooms.

And in answer to the final question from many readers: Yes, educators can legally record and use Super Bowl ads in instruction.

Additional Resources

Check SuperBowl-Ads.com for updates on ads.

AdWeek's 2016 Super Bowl Ad Tracker: www.adweek.com/news/advertising-branding/super-bowl-ad-tracker-everything-we-know-about-2016s-commercials-168657

LESSON 15

Being Savvy About Diet Ad Season

Background

If you're reading this in January, you're probably already getting inundated by promises to remove the fat without sacrificing the calories or breaking a sweat.

After the holidays, the weight-loss/diet industry bombards consumers (including susceptible tweens and teens) with messages on radio, television, and the web. They know that many of us overindulged during the holidays, and they're making promises (most too good to believe) that you can take that weight off fast. But can you? And can you believe everything they say? A little healthy skepticism goes a long way. That is what "media literacy" is all about.

It's not just ads in the media. Check editorial content, too. Magazine covers, many aimed at the female demographic, are on newsstands now. *People Magazine*, for example, always uses the first issue of the New Year to tout celebrity and real-people diets and advice. See an example in the Media Link box below.

Media Link

Show students the 2014 issue *People Magazine* cover which proclaims "Half Their Size" and shows before-and-after photos of dieters: http://frankwbaker.com/mlc/people-magazine-diet-cover.

The Federal Trade Commission (FTC), which oversees advertising, has some very good advice for us: "If you see an ad for a weight-loss product making fantastic claims, keep your money in your pocket."

Fantastic promises are not hard to find. "The easiest diet ever" claims one product; "I lost 89 pounds" says another. Even though this sounds attractive and appealing, can it possibly be true? "Testimonials from individuals are not a substitute for science, and that's what Americans need to understand," said an FTC chair quoted in the news back in 2007.

There are several specific claims the FTC says dieters need to be wary of:

1. You can lose weight without diet or exercise.
2. You can lose weight no matter how much you eat of your favorite foods.
3. You can lose weight permanently; never diet again.
4. You can just take a pill.
5. You can lose 30 pounds in 30 days.
6. Everybody will lose weight.
7. You can lose weight with our diet patch or cream.

To help consumers better cut through the hype, the FTC created a report titled "Red Flag: Bogus Weight Loss Claims" (www.business.ftc.gov/sites/default/files/pdf/bus60-red-flag-bogus-weight-loss-claims.pdf). Using dramatic imaging and bold red pennants, it warned people about the deceptive advertising, offering some strong advice:

> Misleading weight loss advertising is everywhere, preying on consumers desperate for an easy solution. There is no magic bullet when it comes to losing weight. Claims for diet products that promise weight loss without sacrifice or effort are bogus, and in some cases, dangerous.

As the FTC also notes, those before-and-after photos can be highly manipulative. Have you noticed how unhappy the people (usually actors) are and how poor their posture is in the before photos – but how happy and attractive they look in the after?

And then there are the Photoshopped images of celebrities, endlessly tweaked by graphics designers to remove every blemish and sculpt perfect, fat-free bodies. (Does anyone think the Kardashians ever looked quite like this?)

Activity: Diet Ads in the Classroom

So what does this annual avalanche of diet advertising mean to you, the classroom teacher? Use it as yet another "media literacy" teachable opportunity, while also sharpening critical thinking skills.

1. Look for weight-loss ads to share with students. You won't have any problem locating some in many of the magazines you come across during January (and beyond). You can also do a simple Google image search for "diet advertising" and turn up a virtual history of diet ads.

2. Consider using some of this material to teach students not only about persuasive techniques, but also argument writing – an important Common Core standard, as we have discussed. As this blog post (www.vriuvm.org/uncategorized/persuasive-vs-argument-writing) explains, the CCSS expects students to learn how to argue in writing using reasoning and evidence. Applying these standards of argument to diet advertising quickly reveals the difference between persuasion and argument.
3. Have students identify audience, purpose, wording, and visual and audio techniques. This handy two-page document (http://hrsbstaff.ednet.ns.ca/michaelh/H._Michael/Design_Assignments_files/deconstructing%20ads%20handout.pdf) offers good advice for deconstructing print ads. In this lesson plan (www.frankwbaker.com/deconstructing_a_tv_commercial.htm), there is timely advice as well, and a series of questions your students can use that will help them identify the key elements in commercials.
4. Consider the covers of magazines as content to be studied also. Since the Common Core standards position our students as "reading detectives," they should be developing the basic skills to observe covers for layout, design, color, and more, and then provide evidence to prove the intent of the editors.

Additional Resources

I have created a diet ad website (www.frankwbaker.com/dietadvertising) with a multitude of resources for teaching this topic. I invite you to peruse it and consider how it can help you engage your students in some of the most powerfully persuasive messages out there today.

LESSON 16

Studying Black History Through the Vision of Gordon Parks

Background

My mouth was agape as I watched the documentary "Half Past Autumn: The Life and Works of Gordon Parks" (www.youtube.com/watch?v=VyVZTrB5eAw). How could one man, I asked myself, have accomplished so much in one lifetime? In 90 minutes, I learned that the late Gordon Parks had been a poet, photographer, filmmaker, author, composer, and more.

I was curious about Parks after having experienced a new exhibit (www.high.org/Art/Exhibitions/Gordon-Parks-Segregation-Story.aspx) of never-before-seen images from the 1950s and 1960s at Atlanta's High Museum of Art. (Images from the exhibit as well as other education resources can be found here: www.high.org/Educators/Teacher-Resources/Gordon-Parks-Segregation-Story.aspx; also see Figures 6.1–6.3.)

Parks said he used his "camera as a weapon" to reveal a life white Americans rarely saw or understood. His access to important places and events allowed him to document many people, and he had an outlet for his photography and more.

When I am introduced to an important person in American history, I am anxious to share my enthusiasm for them with teachers and students. Not only are his images available for study, but so are his words. He was a prolific writer – and both images and words should be required viewing and reading.

It's unfortunate that Parks' works are not included in many of today's American history and art history textbooks, because they should be. Here is why.

- During the Depression, he was hired by the Franklin Roosevelt administration's Farm Services Administration to be one of those photographers who documented living conditions of people (in this case, in the South) so that those images could awaken American's consciousness and get the New Deal passed.
- He was the first black photographer hired by *Vogue*, the fashion magazine.

Figure 6.1 At segregated drinking fountain, Mobile, Alabama, 1956

Source: Promised gift of the Gordon Parks Foundation

Figure 6.2 Airline terminal, Atlanta, Georgia, 1956

Source: Collection of the Gordon Parks Foundation

- He was the first black photographer to be hired by *LIFE*, the popular culture/current events magazine, covering the Civil Rights movement and the segregation story, among many others.
- He was the first black director hired by a major Hollywood film studio (Paramount) and the first film he produced was his own life story, *The Learning Tree*, based on the book of the same name. He also wrote and directed *Shaft* starring Richard Roundtree.
- He was a prolific writer, authoring almost 20 books in his lifetime, including *A Choice of Weapons*.

A 20th-Century Renaissance Man

Parks had the ability to get his subjects to feel comfortable with him and his camera, whether the subject was street gangs of Harlem or celebrities of the time.

His story is a rags-to-riches one, but along with success came personal problems along the way. In books written about him and in his own accounts, he is frank about his shortcomings. But in the end he is appreciative of the opportunity he had to tell a story. And tell stories he did . . . lots of them.

Activity: Analyzing Parks' Work

Have students choose one of his images to study. For example, "American Gothic" (Figure 6.3) is considered to be one of Parks' signature images from the Depression, when he worked for the Farm Services Administration.

> Ella Watson was a black charwoman who mopped floors in the FSA building. Parks asked her about her life, which she divulged as having been full of misery, bigotry and despair. Parks' simple question, "would you let me photograph you?" and Ella's affirmative response led to the photographer's most recognizable image of all time.
>
> (www.pdngallery.com/legends/parks/mainframeset.shtml)

Display the photo and ask students what they notice. Ask why they think this photograph became symbolic of the treatment of African Americans at that time in history.

Figure 6.3 American Gothic (Ella Watson), Washington, 1942

Source: Library of Congress Prints and Photographs Division http://en.wikipedia.org/wiki/Gordon_Parks#mediaviewer/File:Gordon_Parks_-_American_Gothic.jpg

Additional Resources

Here are some resources about Parks that might be appropriate for your class or school library:

Gordon Parks: How the Photographer Captured Black and White America (Albert Whitman & Company Publishers), 2014.

The Photographs of Gordon Parks: The Library of Congress (GILES Publishing), 2011.

Gordon Parks, *VISIONS: The Images, Words & Music of Gordon Parks* (DVD), 2009.

Gordon Parks, *No Excuses* (Pelican Publishing), 2006.

Children of the Great Depression (HMH Books for Young Readers; Reprint edition), 2010.

Extraordinary African-Americans: From Colonial To Contemporary Times (Children's Press), 2002.

In addition, the Photo District News (PDN) "Legends Online" (http://pdngallery.com/legends/parks/intro_set.shtml) includes Parks' biography, a gallery of images, and video clips of the photographer talking about many of his images.

PBS has a short video segment (http://video.pbs.org/video/2365401193) on Parks from its Independent Lens documentary "Through a Lens Darkly."

LESSON 17

Civil Rights

How Pictures Changed America

Background

Chances arc, you or your students have never heard of Charles Moore. Moore was a photographer whose assignments made him a witness to many historical moments during the Civil Rights movement.

You've no doubt seen the photojournalism of this small-town Alabama native, who began his career working for the Montgomery newspapers. During the 1960s, his powerful images were published in many U.S. newspapers as well as in *LIFE* magazine, the news and popular culture weekly, which devoted dozens of pages to his work.

If your students think a photo can't change history, have them think again. If they thumb through histories of that time period, they'll come across iconic still photographs that shocked the nation and influenced the decisions of important leaders. Moore believed that his photos would cause people to take political action. He was correct. And he wasn't alone.

News photographers, as well as TV news crews, were regular witnesses to the protests and police violence associated with the activities of the movement's leader, Reverend Martin Luther King Jr., capturing his famous oratory and documenting frequent confrontations with white authorities in the segregated South.

It was those images, appearing on the front pages of many newspapers and on the nightly news broadcasts, which helped bring about the Civil Rights Act of 1964, according to U.S. Senator Jacob Javitz (http://bit.ly/2uDEMMd), and set the stage for passage of the 1965 Voting Rights Act.

King was well aware of the power of the image to communicate – perhaps more effectively than any written or spoken word. Events were scheduled by civil rights leaders to take advantage of TV news cameras and broadcast deadlines.

Andrew Young, a key advisor to King, understood the importance of television and photojournalism:

> In the Civil Rights Movement, it was our ability to package a message to illustrate our cause in a 60 second segment on the evening news that was key to our success. We could not have been effective without television.
>
> (www.operationhope.org/pressrelease/nid/1003)

John Lewis and the Selma March

Another civil rights activist, now-U.S. Rep. John Lewis (D-GA), was a young man when he was injured in March 1965 by Southern law enforcement officers. Lewis led the Bloody Sunday march in Selma, where Alabama state troopers attacked peaceful protesters with billy clubs, bullwhips, and tear gas. A photo taken by another Alabama-based photographer, Spider Martin, whose time as a *Birmingham News* staffer parallels Moore's experience, shows Lewis on the ground trying to ward off a blow. (See this *New York Times* story to access Martin's images: http://nyti.ms/2sG8peo.)

The horrific actions in Selma were broadcast on nightly news reports into living rooms across America (http://to.pbs.org/2lcPtBN). Selma's mayor was stunned, admitting, "I didn't understand how big it was until I saw it on television . . . That looked like a war; that went all over the country" (http://bit.ly/2tFumOP).

John Lewis recently recounted many of these incidents in a trilogy of best-selling graphic novels entitled *March*. The books have been honored with a National Book Award as well as by the American Library Association. Teachers of American history and librarians should give serious consideration to acquiring these books, filled with powerful imagery, for their teaching collections. Many of the illustrations echo the work of news photographers.

For more iconic civil rights images associated with Lewis, see the recent PBS documentary *John Lewis – Get in the Way*.

Moore at the Heart of the Action

In summer 1963, Charles Moore was already a veteran of the Civil Rights movement. Moore was present in Birmingham, Alabama when dogs were used by local police to quell peaceful anti-segregation demonstrators. His powerful image, of a dog tearing the pants off one man, made its way into *LIFE* magazine, which at the time was read by half of all Americans (see Media Link box on the next page).

Media Link

Access the award-winning photo here: http://100photos.time.com/photos/charles-moore-birmingham-alabama.

TIME magazine has recognized this photograph as one of the "100 Most Influential Images of All Time." Historian Arthur Schlesinger Jr., referencing the then-Commissioner of Public Safety for the city of Birmingham, said of the image: "The photographs of Bull Connor's police dogs lunging at the marchers in Birmingham did as much as anything to transform the national mood."

Moore, who died in 2010 at age 79, believed his camera was his tool, something more powerful than any gun or knife, because his photographs captured the tension and emotion of everything in the photo's frame. *"I Fight With My Camera"* is a short and compelling documentary about the Civil Rights movement, featuring Moore's images and his own voice, talking about many of his pictures and expressing his feelings during that period. (Teachers might find portions of the 2005 video effective with more mature students. Preview it first.)

In their Pulitzer Prize-winning book *The Race Beat*, noted journalists Gene Roberts and Hank Klibanoff describe how Moore used a short-range lens, forcing himself to get very close to the action as he documented the aftermath of the fire-hose moments. Moore got so close to a stoic-faced man whose hat and shirt were soaking wet that he said he could see drops of water, like tears, coming from the man's eyelids.

At Google Books, you can view the complete May 17, 1963 issue of *LIFE* and see how Moore's fire-hose images and other photos from Birmingham were presented to America in the most popular magazine of the time (http://bit.ly/2szyNvb). The photo spread begins on page 26 and carries the headlines "The Spectacle of Racial Turbulence in Birmingham: They Fight a Fire That Won't Go Out" and "Provocation and Reprisal Widen the Bitter Gulf." As many commentators have noted since, the impact of page after page of these images is difficult to overestimate.

These and other Moore photographs appear in his 1991 book *Powerful Days*, a title I believe should be on the shelf of every school library. Many of these images, and similar ones, show up in American history textbooks and in documentaries teachers might use in February during Black History month (see my recommended resources at the end of this chapter).

Activity: Using These Images with Students

Ask students: How can a single photo influence the viewer? Looking at examples from the work of Charles Moore and other civil rights era photographers, what elements in the images make them stand out from ordinary photographs that might appear in newspapers and magazines? What impact might such images have had on Washington lawmakers and other influential Americans who were witnessing the events in the southern United States from afar? Do the images tell a story without using words? Images like these often provoke emotion – are they "fair reporting"?

Having your students study and analyze such images can be part of important visual literacy lessons. Understanding the context of the images and the events surrounding them is also important in today's political climate, when lessons of the past are not always recalled with clarity.

Additional Resources

My web page: "Images of the Civil Rights Movement":

http://frankwbaker.com/mlc/images-civil-rights-movement

"The Civil Rights Movement from Behind the Lens" (interview with Charles Moore at Southern Scribe):

www.southernscribe.com/zine/culture/Moore_Charles.htm

"Documentary Photography: Civil Rights Through Image and Text" (Lesson plan – Getty Museum):

http://bit.ly/2tjpcWt

"Captioning the Civil Rights Movement" (ReadWriteThink lesson plan):

http://bit.ly/2eCN6bP

February

The first couple of months of the new year are filled with awards shows . . . all of them leading up to the granddaddy . . . the Oscars. Whether you've seen the nominated films are not, you'll have seen the trailers and perhaps read a review about a worthy film. Students love the movies, so here's another chance to engage them. The lessons in this chapter explore the Academy Awards, the language of film, and the symbols of costume design.

LESSON 18

Learning from the Academy Awards

Background

The Super Bowl, which we looked at in Lesson 14, is one of the few "appointment" TV events that's survived 21st-century American digital culture. By which I mean: a television show so iconic that people across the nation plan parties around the media event or watch it together with friends and family just to see what will happen.

The bowl game is history and the annual buzz about the commercials is finally dying down. What's the next mass-audience television event? The Academy Awards.

After the Super Bowl, the Oscars ceremony is the most "appointment-viewed" television program watched by a huge audience in the United States (and around the world). Many of us stop what we're doing to watch it "live," often with other movie and celebrity buffs. Last year's telecast was seen by more than 37 million viewers.

New and novel advertising isn't the big audience draw at the Oscars. Hollywood is. While ads at the last Super Bowl went for $5 million apiece, Entertainment Weekly reported that advertisers were planning to pay a little less than half that (www.ew.com/article/2015/10/15/oscars-ad-rates) for the same 30 seconds on the Oscar telecast in 2016. Of course ABC-TV and its affiliated stations still stand to benefit from the premium prices of commercials (www.thewrap.com/abcs-oscars-advertising-slots-nearly-sold-out). (The Academy also benefits from the domestic and international rights to the "live" broadcast.)

Even though the Oscar broadcast is scheduled for February or March, the buzz about the awards begins well before then. If you follow the trades (*Variety*, *Hollywood Reporter*, *The Wrap*, et al.) then you will have seen the "For Your Consideration" (FYC) full-page advertisements promoting the nominated films, directors, actors, and other categories.

The FYC ads, which also appear in both the *New York Times* and the *Los Angeles Times*, aim to influence the 6,000+ voting members of the Academy of Motion Picture Arts and Sciences and are created by the studios to promote their movies. (See my Teacher's Guide to The Academy Awards, www.frankwbaker.com/mlc/teaching-academy-awards, for ideas on teaching with these ads.)

Hollywood agents are working overtime now – making sure that any nominated client's name gets out there. That person might be scheduled to appear on a syndicated talk show (e.g., Ellen, the Tonight Show with Jimmy Fallon, Jimmy Kimmel LIVE) or profiled in a magazine (such as *Entertainment Weekly, Film Comment*, or *EMPIRE*) or on nationally broadcast programs such as The Today Show or CBS Sunday Morning. Already, news articles featuring many of the nominees have appeared in the mainstream press and on popular culture blogs and websites.

How the Academy's 18 Branches Break Down

It's not just the well-known actors who get publicity (Table 7.1); directors, art directors, costume designers, and even foley artists will be featured because every Academy category (and nomination) is important.

So how do we teach the awards? Start by using them as an opportunity to teach students about film. Choose a nominated film and try the activities below. Students typically view movies passively: the activities below will help train them to view such carefully constructed, motion-oriented media critically. Film and media literacy education demonstrates exactly how to help students "read" the screen and understand the various tools and techniques used by filmmakers.

Activity 1: Making a Movie Poster

Have students study the design of a movie poster. You might ask them to brainstorm answers to the question: what are the quintessential elements that must be in every motion picture poster? Students could also use Glogster or similar software to create their own marketing posters.

Table 7.1 The Academy of Motion Picture Arts and Sciences' 18 branches. Total voting members: 6,261

Actors: 1,138	Documentary: 237	Public relations: 388
Casting directors: 86	Executives: 458	Short films and feature animation: 401
Cinematographers: 227	Film editors: 254	Sound: 437
Costume designers: 115	Makeup artists and hairstylists: 141	Visual effects: 359
Designers: 278	Music: 257	Writers: 392
Directors: 394	Producers: 483	Members at large: 216

Source: *The Hollywood Reporter*.

Activity 2: Reading the Screenplay

Another promotional push by the film studios is to give voting members, and now the public, access to the nominated films' scripts. "Go into the Story" (http://gointothestory.blcklst.com/free-script-downloads) lists several of those screenplays, which can be downloaded and studied in English language arts, history, and film studies.

Activity 3: Check Out the Trailer

Even though many students may not have seen all of the Oscar-nominated films, they can still view the trailers for the films and read about them online. (The nominees' page, http://oscar.go.com/nominees, on the Oscars website includes links to trailers.)

Trailers are considered persuasive texts because they are designed to pique the interest of the audience, sometimes months ahead of a film's release date. Teachers may wish to consider having students create their own trailers (using free software such as iMovie, PhotoStory 3, or Windows Movie Maker). For more on trailers as persuasive texts, see my web page: www.frankwbaker.com/movie_trailers_as_persuasion.htm.

Activity 4: Write About Film

If your students have seen any of the nominated titles, they can be tasked with writing reviews which could be posted online. If students have never written a film review, then this is a perfect opportunity to expose them to sample reviews written by film critics. They can also consider whether a particular review helps or hurts a film's attendance. Students could also look for excerpts from published reviews which have now been incorporated into the marketing poster or commercial for a nominated film.

Before starting a unit on film, you might wish to use these research questions with students:

1. What are the Academy Awards?
2. What organization disseminates them?
3. Who selects which movies get nominated?
4. What are the specific categories of nominated films?
5. Which genres are represented the most? The least?
6. Who gets to vote for the nominated films?

7. How do film studios promote their film(s) to the voting members of the Academy?
8. Does box office revenue have any role in nominated films – in other words, do movies with large audiences have any better chances of getting recognized than films with smaller audiences?
9. Does box office increase after a film wins an Academy Award?
10. Who gets to attend the annual Academy Awards ceremony?
11. Why does this annual film rite get so much attention?

Additional Resources

The Teacher's Guide to the Academy Awards (www.frankwbaker.com/mlc/teaching-academy-awards) and the Language of Film web page (www.frankwbaker.com/language_of_film) both offer educators lesson plans, readings, and recommended texts and videos.

The Academy of Motion Picture Arts and Sciences has produced an excellent series of teacher guides designed to help introduce the Oscar categories (including documentaries) as well as the language of film. Its Teacher Guide Series (www.oscars.org/educational-programs/teachers-guide-series) can be downloaded individually from the Education/Outreach section of its website.

In its online store, the National Council of Teachers of English offers several excellent texts which include lists of recommended films and how to teach them, as well as movie-oriented lesson plans at ReadWriteThink. See also my references here to both visual literacy and film as well as teaching film literacy without the film.

LESSON 19

Exploring the Language of Film

Background

I think it's more important than ever that 21st-century students become "critical viewers" and more "film literate." When students are challenged to "close read" a video/film, they must not only learn how to deconstruct the "media text," but they must also understand and appreciate all of the elements and techniques that are used to create it.

> Films can be read like texts. Their images should be unpacked just as we would unpack the imagery in a written passage. [Students should] think carefully about how visual or aural tools enact, reshape, change, or critique an author's textual expressions.
>
> (Holly Blackford, "The Basics of How to Read a Film," http://teacherweb.com/PA/ParklandHighSchool/MrsTessitore/The-Basics-of-How-to-Read-a-Film.doc)

The Language of the Moving Image

I define the language of the moving image (video/film) as both the *tools* and the *techniques* used to imply or create meaning. Here is my short list of those language elements:

- Cameras (cinematography)
- Lighting
- Audio/sound (includes music)
- Set design
- Post production (editing, special effects)
- Actors (wardrobe, makeup, body language, expressions)

The late film critic Roger Ebert suggested that teachers first consider using film stills (for example, publicity stills) rather than film clips to introduce what he called "frame analysis" (analogous to close reading). Here are some ways to do this in the classroom.

Figure 7.1 Publicity still: *To Kill a Mockingbird*

Activity 1: Analyzing High Angles

Show students how high angles – shooting down on people – takes their power away from them. Show students this publicity still (Figure 7.1) from *To Kill a Mockingbird*. Ask: Do you think the filmmakers are sending a message to the audience with this camera position?

Activity 2: Analyzing Low Angles

Now show students that just as high angles take power away, low angles add power. Display the Hitler still from the documentary *Triumph of the Will* (see Media Link box). Ask students:

1. Where is the camera positioned?
2. How does it make the subject look?
3. What else might a low angle/upward shot of a person signify?

If students easily answered the first and second questions but were stumped by the third, they're not alone. As photographers and cinematographers know, when you shoot up at a person, you make them appear not only larger but also more powerful and commanding than they might normally seem.

Media Link

Here is the still in which documentary filmmaker Leni Riefenstahl famously photographed Adolf Hitler from a low angle in the 1935 propaganda film *Triumph of the Will*: http://bit.ly/2tgp9ee.

Activity 3: Looking at a Filmmaker's Representation of Character

> Filmmakers can use a number of techniques to establish and develop characters. Their choice of camera techniques, acting . . . editing, lighting and sound all contribute to the representation of a character.
>
> (Brett Lamb, "Representation in Film," http://bit.ly/2zngtEL)

Teach students that another way filmmakers communicate to audiences is through the placement of actors within the frame. Consider the farmer, who's come to make payment to Atticus, at the beginning of *To Kill a Mockingbird* (Figure 7.2).

Have students notice not only his clothing but also how he stands at the bottom of the steps and that both Atticus and Scout look down on him, indicating a difference in social class.

You could also teach representation of character through *A Raisin in the Sun*. In 2008, a revival of the Lorraine Hansberry family drama *A Raisin in the Sun* was adapted for television, with rapper-producer-actor Sean Combs in a lead role as the son Walter Younger. (This contemporary version might resonate more with today's students than the black-and-white version with Sidney Poitier as Walter.)

In a pivotal scene (www.youtube.com/watch?v=ybffbxq5Jag), Walter is preparing to walk out of his mother's apartment, even though his wife wants to talk to him. An argument ensues. Notice how the director places daughter-in-law Ruth (portrayed by Audra McDonald) in the middle of the

Figure 7.2 Publicity still: *To Kill a Mockingbird*

frame between mother Lena (portrayed by Phylicia Rashad) and son Walter, representing a key dynamic within the play. See the screen grabs on my website (Media Link below).

Media Link

A *Raisin in the Sun* screen grabs: http://frankwbaker.com/mlc/raisin-in-the-sun.

Common Core Connections

The Common Core makes two specific references to film in the English language arts (ELA) teaching standards.

In 7th grade students are challenged to:

> Compare and contrast a story, drama, or poem to its audio, filmed, staged, or multimedia version, analyzing the effects of techniques unique to each medium (e.g., lighting, sound, color, or camera focus and angles in a film).

In 8th grade students are challenged to:

> Analyze the extent to which a filmed or live production of a story or drama stays faithful to or departs from the text or script, evaluating the choices made by the director or actors.

Activity 4: Comparing a Film Version to a Text

To assist teachers who want to meet these two standards, I recently created this lesson plan (http://frankwbaker.com/mlc/tkam-editing-exercise) which engages students by having them read a passage from Harper Lee's *To Kill a Mockingbird* and compare it to the same scene in the screenplay. Students must also think like a director/cinematographer and decide where and how to position the camera to recreate the scene, which takes place just after the jury has found Tom Robinson guilty. Figure 7.3 on the next page shows how the director set the scene.

Activity 5: Looking at Editing Decisions (Post Production)

When most of us watch film, we're not really aware of all of the techniques filmmakers use. Post-production editing is one of the most powerful, as directors and editors pick and choose which scenes and images will be included in the final creation and how it will all be fitted together. When showing a movie in class, call attention to the editing process and the way it shapes our responses to the film.

Consider the 1997 film *Titanic*. Many students believe this to be a true story, but in fact it's a docudrama, a blend of true and fictional elements. One of the techniques the director, James Cameron, uses to make us think it's all true is the "dissolve" – when one image slowly fades away while another image begins to replace it, often representing a shift in time or location, or both.

One memorable example of this technique: We meet the older Rose at the beginning of *Titanic* and as she reminisces, the dissolve begins, and we move from the present to her past – her memories come alive. Clever directors can also use the dissolve technique to add a sense of reality or truth to their fictions. Note the stills in the Media Link box on the next page.

Figure 7.3 Publicity still: *To Kill a Mockingbird*

Media Link

Titanic stills: www.angelfire.com/ga/wkb/titanic.html.

Have students analyze the moment where the editor chooses to add a dissolve and explain the effect on the viewer.

In a recent edition of his book *The English Teacher's Companion*, author-educator Jim Burke urged teachers to embrace movies, advertising, and other visual media and to find opportunities to use them in instruction. Otherwise, he says, teachers risk their credibility with students.

That's some good food for thought. I hope that this look at the close reading of film feeds your appetite for including media literacy in your approach to close reading and the Common Core.

Additional Resources

I recently created this Language of Film website (http://frankwbaker.com/mlc/language-of-film) to assist educators. It includes links to articles, lesson plans, and resources.

Be sure to visit the Film in the Classroom (http://learning.blogs.nytimes.com/teaching-topics/film-in-the-classroom) index page at the *New York Times* Learning Network to find links to their large collection of articles and resources for teachers and students.

My colleague Heidi Hayes Jacobs and I recently unveiled this Film Canon website (http://filmcanonproject.com). We invite educators who already use film to join (it's free) and contribute to the growing list of films appropriate for the classroom. You'll find recommendations and related materials organized by grade levels (e.g., middle school).

Other Recommended Websites:

Academy of Motion Pictures Arts and Sciences Teacher Guide Series:

www.oscars.org/education-grants/teachers-guide-series

The Columbia Film Language Glossary:

https://filmglossary.ccnmtl.columbia.edu

AFI Screen Education, The 21st Century Educators Handbook:

www.unitedstreaming.com/videos/42845/D2B15956-1279-3B00-CD01B9EA8FD93498.pdf (note: videos that accompany the material in this handbook can be found via YouTube Thinking Film: www.thefilmspace.org/thinking-film).

Screen Education, periodical, Australian Teachers of Media:

www.metromagazine.com.au/screen_ed

Suggested Articles:

"Teachers Look to Film to Foster Critical Thinking":

www.edweek.org/ew/articles/2013/08/15/01film.h33.html

"How to Close Read the Language of Film":

www.middleweb.com/16848/close-read-language-film

"How To Read a Movie":

www.rogerebert.com/rogers-journal/how-to-read-a-movie

"Scriptwriting, the Language of Film and Media Literacy":

http://blogs.slj.com/connect-the-pop/2013/02/movies/scriptwriting-the-languages-of-film-and-media-literacy-teaching-the-oscars-with-frank-baker

"Screenwriting as an ELA Exercise":

http://blogs.ncte.org/index.php/2015/12/screenwriting-as-an-ela-exercise

"Films Inspired by True Events Walk a Tricky Line":

http://articles.latimes.com/2013/nov/21/news/la-en-real-life-stories-20131121

"Focus on Film, Learning It Through the Movies":

http://files.eric.ed.gov/fulltext/ED497090.pdf

Reading the Symbols of Costume Design

Background

Did You See What She Was Wearing?

If anything is important to middle schoolers today, it is their appearance. The clothes they choose to wear communicate their fashion sense (or perhaps lack thereof) as well as their identity. And the media is certainly one of the major influences on what they decide to purchase and wear.

Do you think your students ever notice what the actors wear in the movies? I certainly didn't, until recently.

While I've been teaching the language of film for a while, I've not really spent much time on costume design and how important that is in a movie. But what an actor wears is as important, if not more so, than the camerawork, lighting, sound, and editing.

The Common Core standards for ELA remind students to consider both the techniques used in filmmaking as well as the choices made by directors and actors.

Costumes certainly fall within these areas. Drama and theater teachers, as well as their students, must certainly study costumes. As Oscar-winning director/producer Martin Scorsese says, in many movies "costume is character."

Costume designers for motion pictures say it is the clothes that help not only tell the story, but also communicate the setting and bring a character to life. What would Dorothy be without her red slippers; Indiana Jones without his fedora and whip; Audrey Hepburn without that hat?

Behind those clothes are costume designers, who have their very own category in the Academy Awards.

If you're a fan of the movie awards, you may (or may not) recall some of the films that took home the Oscar for best costume in the past years. (See the Media Link below for an infographic showing the movie and winning costume designer.)

Media Link

Costume design winners: http://frankwbaker.com/mlc/costume-design-winners.

Activity 1: Researching Costume Designers

One teaching suggestion here would be for your students to conduct research into one of the designers listed below, or the designer behind one of their favorite films. (The Internet Movie Database, www.imdb.com, is a great resource for locating film credits. And you'll find a complete list of Oscar winners for costume design at this Wikipedia entry: http://en.wikipedia.org/wiki/Academy_Award_for_Best_Costume_Design.)

Undoubtedly, Hollywood's best-known costume designer was Edith Head. She has been honored with eight Academy Awards (a record), starting with *The Heiress* (1949) and ending with *The Sting* (1974). And she was the subject of a parody. Animators for the 2004 Pixar movie *The Incredibles* paid homage to her by creating the character Edna Mode.

If you're looking for a concise biography of Edith Head and her work in Hollywood, take a look at the video posted here: www.youtube.com/watch?v=iYkdf3IGs38.

The book *Edith Head: The 50 Year Career of Hollywood's Greatest Costume Designer* might also be worth adding to your school library's collection. Students could read about Head and then summarize some of the designer's best-known decisions and the impact she had.

Activity 2: A Closer Look at the Costume Design Process

Websites like Clothes on Film (http://clothesonfilm.com) and *Entertainment Weekly Magazine*'s column Wardrobe Notes (http://popstyle.ew.com/tag/wardrobe-notes) can be valuable teaching resources for helping students to appreciate the process and people behind dressing actors for film roles. So how can you help students better appreciate and recognize costume design when using film in the classroom? The following questions could be used as a starting guide:

1. What's your favorite film and what do you recall about the characters' costumes?
2. Why do you think we seldom notice costumes when viewing films?
3. How do costumes reflect the time period the film was made?
4. Are there times when the costume overshadows the actor wearing it?
5. What makes a costume memorable?

The next time you watch a movie, in the theater, at home, or on some other device, take time to notice what the actors are wearing.

It's not hard to see that helping students build awareness of what an actor or character wears in a movie is part of those "critical viewing skills" we want students to have and appreciate.

Additional Resources

Be sure to see my Language of Film: Costume Design website, http://frankwbaker.com/mlc/language-of-film-costumes, for recent news stories about film costume, lesson plans, and links to recommended books and videos.

March

Can you believe everything you see on the screen? Of course not. But many of our students do. To many of them, everything is true. They don't always apply critical thinking to what they watch. That's why media literacy is so important. Have you noticed lately how many films are "based on a true story"? Hollywood seems to love these, and so do teachers. What follows are my thoughts about teaching with and about these kinds of films and engaging your students in some healthy skepticism. The first lesson is how Hollywood alters history and the second is on documentaries. But it's not just about truth vs fiction; it's also about feeling. Therefore, this section ends with a lesson teaching students to consider how media appeals to our emotions.

LESSON 21

Comparing: History vs Hollywood

Who Gets the Story Right?

Background

In Lesson 22, we will look specifically at docudramas about the media. Here we'll look at docudramas on a broader array of topics to have students consider fact vs fiction – and why that matters. In other words, is it okay for Hollywood to sway from the historical record?

In this excerpt from a *Hollywood Reporter* story about the eagerness to "fact-check" docudramas, the author writes:

> But today we live in the age of Google, when a quick fact-check is just an Internet search away. And so movies – especially movies running the gauntlet of the Oscar-vetting process – can't get away as easily with playing fast and loose with the truth.
>
> (www.hollywoodreporter.com/race/12-years-a-slave-captain-655742)

While historians will tell us that much of history is interpretation of primary source materials – making "truth" somewhat elusive – we know that Hollywood often shows few qualms about mangling timelines, physical locales, and other historical elements that are firmly established in the history books. Are the filmmakers and screenwriters doing anything wrong? *New York Times* film critic A.O. Scott doesn't think so:

> Keep in mind artists of all kinds are supposed to be creative; it's the job of writers, directors, and actors to invent false realities. It's unfair to blame filmmakers if the audience sometimes confuses the real world with movie representations.

And these comments from *TIME* magazine's writers could easily apply to historical accounts as well as fiction:

> Almost any novel's plot must be compressed into a black hole of incident and image. Then there's the challenge any movie faces of

> putting thoughts into words, emotions into gestures, descriptions into actions. And always the adapters must worry not just about satisfying those persnickety readers but also about pleasing the audience ignorant of the book.
>
> (http://content.time.com/time/magazine/article/0,9171,1134742,00.html)

Activity 1: Comparing a Film to a Novel

Many educators already use film adaptations (http://teachingliterature.pbworks.com/w/page/19920348/Film%20or%20TV%20Study%20and%20Adaptations), including having their students "read the novel/watch the film" and do a compare-and-contrast. With the film awards season still fresh in our minds this season, and knowing students love movies, it is a prime time to be teaching this standard.

Many students may have seen one or more of the current crop of docudramas – *Lone Survivor, Saving Mr. Banks, 12 Years A Slave, Captain Phillips, Wolf of Wall Street, Philomena,* and *Mandela,* just to name a few. Or they may be familiar with some of those movies from last year: *Lincoln, Argo, Zero Dark Thirty,* or *Hitchcock.* But how many will have read the books from which these films have been adapted?

No doubt, if they have read the book (or are familiar with the facts of an historical event), then they tend to be more knowledgeable about and can speak to the "differences" as well as "what was omitted from the film." Invariably there will be the debate about which was better: the book or the movie?

Common Core Connections

In English language arts/reading: literature, the Common Core teaching standard "Integration of Knowledge and Ideas" (for 8th grade) says:

> CCSS.ELA-Literacy.RL.8.7: Analyze the extent to which a filmed or live production of a story or drama stays faithful to or departs from the text or script, evaluating the choices made by the director or actors.

Activity 2: Is It Okay for Hollywood to Alter the Truth?

Read and discuss with students one or two of these articles on whether it matters if films are historically accurate:

- Fact Checking the Movies: Announcing Truth Teller for Trailers, www.washingtonpost.com/blogs/fact-checker/wp/2014/02/24/fact-checking-the-movies-announcing-truth-teller-for-trailers.

- Does Anybody Care if Movies Are Historically Accurate? http://forward.com/articles/192973/who-cares-if-movies-are-historically-accurate/?p=all
- ABSCAM Con Man: "American Hustle" Wrong, Jennifer Lawrence Too Hot, http://abcnews.go.com/Blotter/abscam-con-man-american-hustle-wrong-jennifer-lawrence/story?id=22720761
- How Accurate Is *The Monuments Men*? www.slate.com/blogs/browbeat/2014/02/10/the_monuments_men_true_story_fact_checking_the_george_clooney_matt_damon.html
- Fact Checking *Lone Survivor*: www.salon.com/2014/01/17/lone_survivor_a_fact_check_partner
- The True Story of *12 Years A Slave*: http://entertainment.time.com/2013/10/18/the-true-story-of-12-years-a-slave
- The Forgotten History Behind *12 Years A Slave*: http://uk.movies.yahoo.com/forgotten-history-behind-12-years-slave-031913709.html
- Just How True Are Hollywood's "True Stories"? http://tinyurl.com/lgg2x8l.
- Films Inspired by True Events Walk A Tricky Line: http://articles.latimes.com/2013/nov/21/news/la-en-real-life-stories-20131121
- Hollywood vs history: A lot of last year's hit movies have tackled real-life events. Two *New York Times* film critics consider how to watch a "historical" movie (NYT UPFRONT): www.thefreelibrary.com/Hollywood+vs.+history:+a+lot+of+this+year%27s+hit+movies+have+tackled...-a0324981284
- Text, Lies and Celluloid: http://business.highbeam.com/416338/article-1G1-141091493/text-lies-and-celluloid-does-film-take-book-end-its

Finally, although not based on historical events, *Gravity* also garnered a good deal of criticism (and defense) from scientists and science geeks: Here's what *Gravity* gets right and wrong about space: www.washingtonpost.com/blogs/wonkblog/wp/2013/10/21/heres-what-gravity-gets-right-and-wrong-about-space.

Additional Resources

Further Articles on the Accuracy of Films

"The Wolf of Wall Street: The True Story":

http://entertainment.time.com/2013/12/26/wolf-wall-street-true-story

"Captain Phillips: Movie vs True Story (History vs Hollywood)":

www.historyvshollywood.com/reelfaces/captain-phillips.php

"The Real Mandela vs. The Movie Version":

www.salon.com/2013/12/07/the_real_mandela_vs_the_movie_version

"Searching for Philomena's Real Son":

www.nytimes.com/2014/01/12/fashion/Philomena-True-Story-Michael-Hess.html

LESSON 22

Analyzing the Media Through Docudramas

Background

What makes movies about the media so appealing? For as long as there have been movies, the media and the subjects they cover have been popular Hollywood topics. And why not?: many of us pay attention not only to the news but also to the media themselves.

What do these movies, past and present, have in common? They're all docudramas. They are not documentaries and they are not true dramas. The docudrama borrows from both genres.

Do your students know that when they watch docudramas, they're not watching history as it actually happened? Do they understand the "artistic license" that movie-makers use when they contract to take an historical event and condense it into a two-hour film?

These movies are not just for the journalism classroom. Every teacher who is concerned about the past, present, and future of the media could use these films as teachable moments.

What follows is not an exhaustive list, but it nonetheless includes some noteworthy movies with media as the central focus:

Docudramas about Media

- *Network* (1976): A network anchorman complains about the trivialization of news and starts to lose his hold on reality. (Who can forget the anchorman's proclamation: "I'm mad as hell and I'm not going to take this anymore!")
- *All the President's Men* (1976) follows *Washington Post* reporters (portrayed by Robert Redford and Dustin Hoffman) as they investigated the Watergate break-in and how their subsequent stories led to the resignation of President Nixon.
- *Broadcast News* (1987): A film that critic Roger Ebert wrote was as "knowledgeable about the TV news-gathering process as any movie ever made."
- *Quiz Show* (1994) profiles the early TV quiz show scandal that led to a Congressional investigation.
- *The Insider* (1995) follows former tobacco executive Jeffrey Wigand (played by Russell Crowe) who is courted by CBS's 60 Minutes to make public Big Tobacco's secrets.

- *Wag the Dog* (1997) profiles consultants who whip up fake news to cover up a presidential candidate's sex scandal.
- *Good Night and Good Luck* (2005): George Clooney's tribute to broadcast journalist Edward R. Murrow as the CBS reporter challenged Senator Joseph McCarthy's Communist witch-hunt techniques.
- *The Social Network* (2010) portrays the birth, struggle, and development of Facebook as the new social media platform.
- *Nightcrawler* (2014) follows a news cameraman (Jake Gyllenhaal) as he works the night shift to photograph news, often crossing ethical boundaries, to help his employer get higher ratings in the highly competitive Los Angeles TV news market.
- *Our Brand Is Crisis* (2015) is a drama featuring Sandra Bullock as a political media consultant who finds a challenge in trying to transform the image of a candidate running for president of Bolivia.
- *Truth* (2015) stars Robert Redford as CBS journalist Dan Rather who in 2008 challenged President George W. Bush's National Guard service record, but whose reputation (and that of his producer) were damaged by the use of questionable sources.
- *Spotlight* (2015) profiles the *Boston Globe* journalists as they pursued allegations of sexual abuse by Catholic church clergy.
- *Trumbo* (2015) stars Bryan Cranston as Dalton Trumbo, the Hollywood screenwriter who was blacklisted as part of the McCarthy-era Communist witch-hunts.

So what are the implications for the classroom? As I have written previously, Common Core middle-grade English language arts standards make specific references to the techniques used in making movies, as well as the decisions made by directors and actors. Whether it's an English teacher using a Shakespeare film or a history teacher using a docudrama, all students need to understand and appreciate the decisions and techniques movie-makers use when they create compelling stories on film. Ask students to consider how a particular film or scene might have been altered to make a subject or person appear better on-screen.

Activity 1: Fact Checking an Event

If you're using films about the media, you might want to first have students conduct background research into the facts behind the media or media event. It's a no-brainer to locate reliable information, for example about the *Washington Post*'s role in reporting on the Watergate scandal. Students could investigate if a particular film scene (e.g. Watergate reporters meeting a secret source in a parking garage) is portrayed accurately.

For the release of *Good Night and Good Luck*, FilmEducation.org produced this film study guide (www.filmeducation.org/pdf/film/GoodNightGoodLuck.pdf) designed to help students dig deeper into Murrow, McCarthy, and the issues the film addresses. RTNDA, the Radio TV News Director's Association, also produced a study guide – excerpts can be found here: https://seps.wikispaces.com/file/detail/Good+night+and+good+luck+study+guide.docx.

For every film that is released "based on true events," there are plenty of legitimate news stories, blog posts, or social media postings that attempt to pull back the curtain on what the filmmakers got right and what they might have altered and why. Challenge your students to find news sources that are pulling back the curtain on the current crop of docudramas.

Teaching Tip: You don't have to wait for the film to be released: you can use the film's trailer to familiarize students with the narrative, characters, conflict, and more. I've created a special website with advice and resources for teaching trailers as persuasive texts: www.frankwbaker.com/mlc/movie-trailers-as-persuasive-texts.

In summary, docudramas can be an effective medium in both English language arts and social studies classes to explore many areas of curriculum, including creative and persuasive writing, current events, historical perspectives, and filmmaking itself.

Additional Resources

Filmeducation.org contains further resources on using film, including docudramas, in the curriculum.

LESSON 23

How Media Appeals to Our Emotions

Background

A photo of a starving child in an ad. A sad-looking dog shown in a cage at an animal shelter. That Hallmark commercial that touches your heart. What do they all have in common? They're all designed to appeal to our emotions.

What role does emotion play in media messages, and how can educators help students recognize this powerful force?

The ad industry now identifies four key human emotions: happy, sad, afraid/surprised, and angry/disgusted (http://bit.ly/2ufBakd). Keep these in mind as you consider helping students connect an emotion with a particular message.

Unruly, which ranks the most viral ads each year, found that the most-shared ads of 2015 relied heavily on emotional content, specifically friendship, inspiration, warmth, and happiness (http://bit.ly/2tgaLT0).

One of my favorite media literacy questions comes into play here: What techniques do media producers employ to make a message credible or believable?

Techniques involve everything from camera angles to color, music, the actors' expressions, editing, and so much more. Do your students understand these media techniques? Would they recognize them if they saw them?

Emotion in Political Advertising

In early 2017, House Minority Leader Nancy Pelosi admitted that Donald Trump resonated better with the voters than Hillary Clinton leading up to the November 2016 election. "He had the emotional connection," she said in this *Washington Post* story, adding, "and that always is an advantage in the campaign" (http://wapo.st/2zmWCp3).

In his book *The Political Brain*, author Drew Westen confirms "the data from political science are crystal clear: people vote for the candidate who elicits the right feelings, not the candidate who presents the best arguments." In a 2007 interview, Westen made the case that one political party communicates better than the rest: "Republicans understand that you have to talk to people about their values first or make an emotionally compelling case for them to be listening to you in the first place" (www.abc.net.au/news/2007-08-25/appealing-to-voters-emotions/650396).

In the 2004 race for the White House, the *New York Times* showed examples from both the Democrats and the Republicans to demonstrate how emotion was being used in their ads. See the infographic noted in the Media Link box below.

Media Link

Political ads appealing to voters' emotions: http://nyti.ms/2swZ65f.

Additional Resources

The website "The Living Room Candidate" is a good place to start. You can stream ads from presidential campaigns between 1952 and 2016.

Campaigning for Hearts and Minds: How Emotional Appeals in Political Ads Work, by Ted Brader (2006).

Fear as a Persuader

In many presidential campaign ads, fear has been used as a powerful persuasive technique. Do you know about Lyndon Johnson's "Daisy" ad against opponent Barry Goldwater (https://en.wikipedia.org/wiki/Daisy_(advertisement))? A little girl is shown counting as she pulls petals from a flower, then a military-sounding voice begins a countdown. As Johnson's voice hints that a Republican win could mean all-out war, the viewer sees several nuclear explosions. (The ad was broadcast only once by the campaign, as Goldwater complained to the White House, but it has lived on in political ad history and online.)

Polls taken after the ad aired (and was re-broadcast by news organizations) confirmed that Americans feared that if Goldwater were elected, he would be more likely to get the U.S. involved in a nuclear war (http://nyti.ms/2sDetUK).

Since the Daisy ad, fear has become commonplace in presidential advertising. Alternet.org has highlighted some of the most memorable fear-invoking ads, streamed in this 2015 article, including "Willie Horton" (George W. Bush), "Teach Your Parents" (Walter Mondale), and Hillary Clinton's "3 AM Call."

Would your students recognize fear as one of the most powerful of the media techniques? We can also find fear in product advertising. Good examples are home security-oriented commercials for ADT, Brinks, etc. or the famous (and much-parodied) "I've fallen and I can't get up" ad from medical alarm company LifeCall. Often, public service announcements also use fear, like the famous "This is your brain on drugs" ad.

Activity 1: Analyzing Fear-Based Ads

This YouTube page shows a commercial for cell phones: www.youtube.com/watch?v=rb9XVKSb1XU. It shows a woman stranded on the side of the road at night "in the middle of nowhere" because her car has broken down. It uses almost every one of the "languages of moving images," and the activity that follows helps students identify them. You may need to let them know that it's a commercial from the 1990s, when most people *didn't* have cell phones.

1. Before you let students see the commercial, ask them to close their eyes and simply listen as you play it. At the conclusion, have them open their eyes and make a list of everything they heard. Allow them to share. You might even create a long list on a board or projector so that everyone can see what's shared.
2. Then, before playing it a second time (this time with their eyes open), ask them to consider the question: other than a product (cell phones), what else is being sold? Play the spot again and survey them about what else may be sold. (They may not get it, but the answer is fear.)
3. Ask students: How is fear shown in the ad? Consider the setting, the camera angles, the lighting, the facial expression, the suspenseful music, the narrator's tone, the sound effects, and more – all of these are the languages of the moving image.

The Emotional Role of Music

One cannot overestimate the role music plays in media productions. Moviemakers, for example, carefully choose a musical collaborator – someone who can create the right music for the right mood or scene.

Composer John Williams scared millions of us when we first watched the film "Jaws" on the big screen. But what would that film have felt like without music? Actor Richard Dreyfuss demonstrated this in a short video from the PBS "Boston Pops" series (https://www.youtube.com/watch?v=-fnq1s-babs).

Those who study music know, for example, that major chords and notes can connote happiness, while minor notes/chords can promote stressful or sad feelings.

Activity 2: Considering the Power of Music

Here are a few examples of emotional music. These are brief YouTube productions, with no images – simply music for your students to listen to and then discuss what they think the music conveys.

Music for Media: Emotion 1: http://bit.ly/2swYtIZ

Music for Media: Emotion 2: http://bit.ly/2t7whLv

Poll your students on music they might recall from a favorite film or two. What was on the screen while the music was playing? How did that music make them feel?

Additional Resources

How Film Scores Play With Our Brains (video):

http://bit.ly/1XcOkKq

Emotion and the Film Scores:

www.e-filmmusic.de/articlc1.htm.

The Undeniable Impact of Music in Film:

http://bit.ly/2uzN3kg

SCORE: A Film Music Documentary (2017):

www.score-movie.com

Activity 3: Locating Emotion in Print Ads

1. Ask students to locate a static ad from a magazine, newspaper, or online site that demonstrates emotion. (The Ad Council website PSACentral has downloadable print ads from many of its campaigns.) What techniques do print ad producers use to convey sadness, happiness, anger, excitement, fear, and more?
2. Then ask them to choose a product or service and create a print or digital ad or a commercial using one of the emotional techniques of persuasion. You'll find some tips in this article at the Center for Digital Education: www.centerdigitaled.com/artsandhumanities/How-to-Create-the-Perfect-Public-Service-Announcement.html. Digital ads are often made

in a "slider" format. (Here's a simple example: http://static.raysweather.com/ad/banners/banner_374.gif.) Students might make three slides that run/loop in sequence.

Media literacy education is more important than ever. Engaging students in a close reading analysis and deconstruction of media texts (ads, TV, film) is just one more way to demonstrate that educators value popular culture and recognize its role in creating 21st-century critical thinkers and learners.

Additional Resources

Georgia Tech study: The more emotional a tweet, the higher the credibility rating (March 2017):

http://bit.ly/2tGEasI

Want to know more about emotions and advertising? Consider having your students read these two articles: "How Brands Use Feelings to Get People to Buy" (http://bit.ly/2ufBakd) and "How Emotions Influence What We Buy" (http://bit.ly/1O2Y8g7).

April

Sports are on my mind this month. The Major League Baseball season kicks off. The NBA playoffs are underway, and recently teams have started making deals that will result in advertising placed on players' jerseys. Bring these topics into the classroom to spark discussion!

LESSON 24

Examining Product Placement

Background

To advertise or not to advertise? That was the question. If you're the National Basketball Association, you opt to advertise.

In case you hadn't heard: NBA players are sporting ads on their jerseys starting with the 2017–18 season.

The ads aren't big and splashy; they take the form of a 2.5-inch by 2.5-inch patch.

Media Link

Here's an example of an ad on an NBA player's jersey: www.middleweb.com/wp-content/uploads/2016/06/bb-jersey-kia.png.

The NBA's commissioner predicted the ads are worth about $100 million a year. (The league's total revenue for 2017–18 is predicted to be $7 billion!) The NBA makes most of its money from its broadcasting contracts.

Do you or your students even care when millions of dollars are at stake?

Do you or your students take the time to consider whether product placement is a good idea or not? In this lesson, I offer you some ideas for consideration.

Analyzing ads helps meet the Common Core English language arts standards for argument. "Ads are, after all, arguments," says rhetoric professor Renee Shea. "As such, they engage students in critical thinking about claims, assumptions, counterargument, types of appeals, logical fallacies, and audience – basic elements of rhetoric" (https://filmandmedia12.wikispaces.com/Teaching+Rhetoric+Using+Advertisements,+Canonical+Texts,+and+Film).

But these aren't just any ads – they're not in a magazine or on TV and they can't be streamed on YouTube and studied later: they're ads on clothes. Many middle school students are already walking advertisements mostly for clothes and shoe brands. (Do they realize that?)

Ads on screens have become known as "branded entertainment" or "product placement," and they exist just about everywhere, but most are prevalent today in movies and television. The idea is simple: put the ad inside the content (as opposed to a commercial which resides outside the content) and the audience won't be likely to skip (fast-forward) past it. When an actor actually holds or uses the product, it becomes a "celebrity testimonial" and can influence consumer purchasing decisions.

Media Link

Here's an example of Oreos digitally inserted into the TV show *Friends*: https://productplacementfun.files.wordpress.com/2013/11/friends.jpg.

In the case of *Friends*, the product is virtual – it's been electronically placed into the scene. This digital insertion technology is used in baseball games where ads are superimposed on top of a green screen behind home plate.

In a movie or TV show, the actual product might be seen on-camera for anywhere from a few seconds to a few minutes, depending on the contractual agreement between the advertiser and the producer of the program. In an NBA game, with the camera focused on the players, the "ad" most likely will be on the screen for a much longer period of time.

Activity: Teaching Students to Analyze Product Placement

1. You might start by posing the following questions for students to consider (Table 9.1):

Table 9.1 Media literacy questions for students to consider

Media literacy/critical thinking questions:	Answers:
What is product placement and how does it work?	Students could research this.
Who makes up the audiences for NBA games?	Students could research this.
Who made the NBA decision regarding jersey ads?	NBA's Board of Governors
Who benefits (and who does not) from the ads on jerseys?	50% of the money from uniform ad deals is kept by teams, while the other 50% goes into a revenue-sharing pot. (http://espn.go.com/nba/story/_/id/14762701/nba-owners-discuss-league-proposal-put-advertisements-jerseys)

2. Ask students on which TV programs they might expect to find product placement (e.g., might *The Amazing Race* lend itself to travel products or services?).
3. When we consider just sports programming, for example, it's easy to spot ads during any NASCAR broadcast. The cars and the driver's uniforms are full of product logos. But is advertising in other sports so prevalent? Assign students another sport: tennis, hockey, baseball, football, soccer, golf, etc. You might ask students to watch a typical broadcast and document ad or logo placement in, say, 15 minutes of a given sport – noting each ad/logo and how much time (seconds or minutes) the advertised product was on-screen.
4. Have them conduct an "image search" of other sports and present their findings. Which sport or sports appear to have more ads on-screen than the others?
5. What about those advertisements inside and outside your own city or school sports arenas and stadiums? Have students noticed those? Did they ever consider the placement or appropriateness of these ads and who benefits?
6. Another idea is to divide the class in two: one group researches the "pros" of product placement in TV and film while the other investigates the downsides. This writer for Forbes (www.forbes.com/sites/lancemadden/2012/07/20/pros-and-cons-corporate-ads-on-nba-jerseys-may-debut-in-2012-13-season/#28d894e16ad7) dives into some of the pros and cons, but I am willing to bet your students might go much further with this topic.

Additional Resources

Product Placement News:

www.huffingtonpost.com/news/product-placement

Product Placement News:

http://productplacement.biz/category/product-placement

Everything You Should Know About Hidden Product Placement (Infographic):

www.themarysue.com/wp-content/uploads/2011/11/Product+Placement-1.png#geekosystem

The Sneakiest Product Placements in Entertainment (Infographic):

www.amazinginfographics.com/wp-content/uploads/2012/09/sneakiest-products-infographic2.jpg

Brand Hype:

www.brandhype.org

Commercial Alert:

www.commercialalert.org

Campaign for Commercial Free Childhood:

www.commercialfreechildhood.org

LESSON 25

Noticing the Power of Branding

Background

Have you watched a major pop culture event on your TV or mobile screen and seen all of those celebrities who stop along the red carpet at a precise point, to have their pictures taken by the paparazzi?

Here's a link to an image of actress Jessica Chastain posing at the 2013 Screen Actors Guild (SAG) award venue. Do you notice anything other than the actress?

Media Link

Jessica Chastain at the SAG awards: www.today.com/entertainment/best-quotes-stars-sag-awards-red-carpet-1C8134865.

In the case of the SAG award photo, the broadcast network TNT is visible in the background, as is AFTRA, the union that represents film, television, and radio artists. Even when some part of a brand's name may be blocked, it's usually repeated many times and we all know what it is.

Pop culture is not alone. Every major sporting event now includes major sponsorships and advertising outside and inside the venue. A quick look at the PGA (golfing) schedule finds: the Honda Classic; the Valspar Championship; and the Arnold Palmer Invitational Presented by MasterCard, just to name a few.

Every major sports stadium now has a brand name attached to it. The most recent Super Bowl game was played at MetLife Stadium in East Rutherford, New Jersey. (MetLife, of course, is the huge insurance company with the blimp that's attached its name to Charles Schultz's *Peanuts* characters for many years.)

NASCAR and soccer are just two of the other major sports where advertising and brands run rampant. There is practically nowhere you can look and *not* see an ad at a NASCAR race!

All of this is to say: somebody is after your eyeballs . . . and thus your attention (and maybe your devotion to the brand). No brand name is there by accident: some corporation paid to make sure it was there. In 2017, product placement is a multibillion-dollar business, pushing out into every aspect of media-related lives, including Facebook, Twitter, Skype, and other popular digital services.

American Idol was one of the first reality TV series to feature cups of the soft drink product Coke, visible on the judges' tables.

At the time, a vice-president for Coke was quoted in the news as saying the placement was more valuable than a 30-second commercial.

Now we have *virtual* ads that show up in sporting events. Using special effects generated in a TV control room, an ad can be placed virtually anywhere on the field. People sitting inside the stadiums don't see the Budweiser ads in the example in the Media Link box below – they are created specifically for the much larger television audience.

Media Link

You can show students these examples of ads at sporting events:

Soccer: http://bit.ly/2t7rEAP.
Baseball: http://atmlb.com/2sx3Ffl.

Activity: Where Is Branding Placed and Why?

So what does all of this mean? And if you're a classroom teacher, why should you care?

Today's young people are the media generation: they pay attention to television, movies, sports, music, and more. But oftentimes, I am told by the educators I work with, they don't watch with any critical viewing skills. They tend to believe everything they see, read, and hear. They're certainly not asking: *why was that ad in the background?* Or, *is that really in the stadium or pasted on the video to influence me?* A major objective of media literacy education, now recognized by many national organizations, is to get our young people thinking critically about why a particular message might have been placed where it was and who benefits from that placement. We may always be consumers, but we can become savvy consumers through media literacy education.

AUTHORSHIP:	Who made this message?
PURPOSE:	Why was it made? Who is the target audience and how do you know?
ECONOMICS:	Who paid for this?
IMPACT:	Who might benefit from this message? Who might be harmed by it? Why might this message matter to me?
RESPONSE:	What kinds of actions might I take in response to this message?
CONTENT:	What ideas, values, information, and/or points of view are overt? Implied? What is left out of this message that might be important to know?
TECHNIQUES:	What techniques are used? Why were those techniques used? How do they communicate the message?
INTERPRETATIONS:	How might different people understand this message differently? What is my interpretation of this and what do I learn about myself from my reaction or interpretation?
CONTEXT:	When was this made? Where or how was it shared with the public?

Figure 9.1 Media literacy questions

Source: National Association for Media Literacy Education (NAMLE)

Introducing the concept of "product placement" (using pop culture images and sporting events) is a great way to jump-start your students' critical viewing and media literacy skills. Give students opportunities to ask the media literacy questions above (see Figure 9.1). These questions can help make students smarter, wiser, and more engaged communicators in a 21st-century world.

Additional Resource

The NAMLE questions can also be found here:

www.frankwbaker.com/namle-questions.jpg

May

Visual literacy is increasingly important in education and in the daily lives of young people. Most of what they see today passes right past them because they don't all possess the skills to read and understand how images communicate. What follows are three lessons covering additional areas of visual literacy. You'll help students understand messages in popular magazines, interpret iconic news images, and understand the role of celebrity in raising our awareness.

Understanding Media Messages in Popular Magazines

Background

We all have magazines at home and at school. They have a high student engagement factor in the classroom and are proving to be a very effective way to teach visual literacy, media literacy, and a host of Common Core standards.

It all started for me when NBA basketball player LeBron James adorned the cover of several magazines, published within weeks or months of each other. Using Google's image search function, it was easy to locate and download cover images for the activity I planned with a large group of teachers. I created a one-page handout, which you can find at the Media Link below.

Media Link

LeBron James covers: http://frankwbaker.com/mlc/lebron-james-magazine-covers.

Once I selected these three images, I began to consider the kinds of questions I wanted educators (or students) to think about when analyzing and deconstructing the covers.

Activity: You Be the Detective

Much has been written recently about students becoming "detectives," and part of this investigative work means knowing what questions to ask. The Common Core standards emphasize "close reading" analysis, with the emphasis being on student observation (what do you see?) and evidence (what in the text makes you think that?).

Similarly, both media and visual literacy encourage critical inquiry. Visual literacy is also quite evident in CCS-English Language Arts in grades 2–6.

So the questions I posed to teachers about the LeBron covers, and which you can pose to your students, are these:

1. Who is the audience for each magazine? What are the clues?

Every magazine targets a specific group of people. In the ad business, it's known as demographics. If students are unfamiliar with the exact target audience of a periodical, they can certainly begin to study the types of ads and products contained in the magazine and make some educated guesses. The bits of "teaser" text on the covers also offer clues about the audience editors and publishers are trying to hook.

2. What one or two adjectives would you choose to describe how he looks on the cover?

This is relatively easy for most covers. In the LeBron examples, he looks much more serious (his "game face") on the *Sports Illustrated* cover than he does on either *Black Enterprise* or *Gentleman's Quarterly*. Students can be prompted to explain why they believe each magazine chose the particular "look" they did.

3. Magazine covers are also considered advertisements. What techniques does each of the publications use to sell themselves to their readers?

I'm not sure how many teachers even approach teaching covers as advertisements for a product (the magazine itself), or how many students ever consider this question. But let's be honest: magazine covers *are* ads that, if done well, lure us in. They use specific techniques (layout, color, font size, images, and more) to get us to pick them up whether we're in the checkout line at the grocery store or just browsing at the local Barnes & Noble bookstore.

Covers may even be considered informational texts, with headlines and other details designed to engage the reader. Of course, the ultimate purpose of the cover is to get the consumer to purchase it, so the entire cover might also be considered a persuasive text. A good follow-up question here might be: what on the cover makes you want to buy it?

4. Notice LeBron's non-verbal facial expressions; what do they say/reveal to you?

Imagine you're the photographer responsible for taking the shot that's going to grace the cover of each of these magazines. How will you position the subject and what expression do you want him to convey to the reader? Since students rarely study expression (outside of drama or public speaking), this is another opportunity for the teacher to call attention to the importance of expression in communication. How different is his smile or the cast of his eyes on the fashion cover and the business cover, for example?

5. If you could read only one of these publications, which would it be and why? In other words, which is most appealing?

Ok, here's five dollars. Which magazine are you going to purchase and why? What do you hope to gain by reading the magazine you chose? Why did you choose one over the others? What demographic are *you* a part of?

Teaching Tip: You can extend this lesson with one additional critical thinking activity. Pose this question to students: Who benefits from your purchase of a magazine? Students should brainstorm, creating a long list of people and companies that benefit from magazine purchases. Obviously, many people, beyond the advertisers themselves and the store, benefit. (For example, does the National Basketball Association benefit from *Sports Illustrated*?)

Students might also consider Media Literacy Core Concept #1 – "All media messages are constructed," followed by the key questions: "How was this created? Who made this message?" (in this case, the magazine).

Graphic design understanding comes into play here, as each publication employs artists and designers to use techniques sure to appeal to the reader. Students will also have to dive deep into a magazine to determine what company is responsible for creating the magazine. The largest companies, like Conde Nast, publish magazines for widely varied demographic/interest groups. (The remaining media literacy concepts, http://medialiteracy3.files.wordpress.com/2011/05/5coreconcepts.jpg, and questions, www.frankwbaker.com/namle-questions.jpg, should also be used here.)

Some Final Thoughts

Now that many magazines have migrated online and onto tablets and e-readers, students should also consider how reading from a screen differs from print, and how the producers of those magazines have altered the traditional magazine cover design and added interactive, multimedia elements. (Online participation allows publishers to collect a vast amount of data about user interests, unthinkable before the Internet.)

After students have analyzed magazines, you might give them opportunities to create their own magazine cover. Just googling the phrase "create your own magazine cover" brings up a host of websites available for you to consider using with your students.

Using magazines to teach Common Core standards is another way of reaching your students, especially those considered "at risk." When you introduce a cover featuring someone they instantly recognize (e.g. singer, movie star, celebrity, sports figure), your students are more likely to be engaged and want to tell you what they know about the subject. So, you'll be opening the door to meeting them where they are.

Additional Resources

Websites

Reading The Pictures:

www.readingthepictures.org

What's Going on in This Picture?:

http://learning.blogs.nytimes.com/category/lesson-plans/whats-going-on-in-this-picture

The Transformative Image: The Power of A Photograph For Social Change: The Death of Aylan:

www.revistacomunicar.com/indice-en/articulo.php?numero=47-2016-03

Faking It: An Interactive Quiz About Digital Alterations:

www.metmuseum.org/metmedia/interactives/adults-teachers/faking-it

IVLA Visual Literacy Resources:

http://ivla.org/new/visual-literacy-resources

Visual Thinking Strategies and the Common Core Standards (video):

https://vimeo.com/81688821

Articles

"Media Literacy: How To Close Read Infographics":

www.middleweb.com/34963/media-literacy-how-to-close-read-infographics

"Photo-Detectives: Connecting the Cross-Cultural With the Cross-Curricular":

http://blogs.edweek.org/edweek/global_learning/2016/01/photo-detectives_connecting_the_cross-cultural_with_the_cross-curricular.html

"Is That Chart Saying What You Think It's Saying?":

https://hbr.org/2016/01/is-that-chart-saying-what-you-think-its-saying

"2015: The Year in Pictures: How We Made The Cut":

http://lens.blogs.nytimes.com/2015/12/22/times-year-in-pictures-2015-meaghan-looram-jeffrey-scales-lens

"Every Picture Tells A Story: Photographers Discuss The Best News Photos":

www.ibtimes.co.uk/every-picture-tells-story-photographers-discuss-best-news-photos-2015-1532587

"Eye Tracking Research Reveals Which Types of Visuals Actually Get the Message Across":

http://phys.org/news/2015-11-eye-tracking-reveals-visuals-message.html

"Infographics Lie. Here's How to Spot the B.S.":

www.fastcodesign.com/3024273/infographic-of-the-day/infographics-lie-heres-how-to-spot-the-bs

Reading and Interpreting Iconic News Images

Background

Even before the invention of photography, certain images gained iconic status in human culture. Our history and art textbooks are full of examples, and many of them are etched in our memories.

Benjamin Franklin's "Join or Die" snake image (Figure 10.1), said to be the first American political cartoon, originally appeared during the French and Indian War, was repurposed by Paul Revere in 1775, and continues to be a powerful representation of the movement toward U.S. independence and nationhood. More recent visual texts, from the Hindenburg disaster, to Iwo Jima, to MLK's "I Have a Dream" speech, to the haunting images of September 11, help us understand what "iconic" means in terms of cultural memory and messaging.

Figure 10.1 Benjamin Franklin's "Join or Die" political cartoon

Iconic Images in Today's News

I thought about these kinds of images as one photo in particular went "viral" following the unrest in the city of Baltimore in April 2015. Social media were flooded with photos, some taken by news photographers, but many others by people on the streets. One of those images apparently touched a nerve for those who saw it. It shows a young boy, his arms full of water bottles, attempting to hand one to a policeman, wearing riot gear and standing on line.

According to Yahoo News, the photo was posted to Facebook by Bishop M. Cromartie, a senior pastor at Baltimore's Prophetic Deliverance Ministries. Several sources reported that the boy was acting on his own initiative.

It was "one of the many pictures that I captured today in the midst of helping clean up the city," Cromartie commented. "It speaks volumes." The photo went "viral" with tens of thousands of others posting it and commenting on it (http://news.yahoo.com/viral-photo-sends-message-of-hope-from-a-ravaged-baltimore-033244863.html?soc_src=mail&soc_trk=ma).

A good question for media-savvy students might be: How does this image make you feel . . . especially since many other images (of violence) seemed to receive more prominence during the events?

To find other images from the Baltimore riots, see this compilation (www.usatoday.com/story/news/nation/2015/04/27/baltimore-riots-photos/26488707) by USA Today. The Newseum in Washington, D.C. has posted April 28 newspaper front pages (www.newseum.org/2015/05/01/the-baltimore-riots-newseum-resources) along with lessons on how news companies report protests, and materials on several earlier Civil Rights protests. *TIME* magazine used the dramatic photo (by aspiring photographer Devin Allen) on the cover of its May 11 issue to raise important social questions.

Why Do Some Images Become Icons?

What makes an image iconic? Is it the composition, the quality, the context . . . or is it something else?

"I think the most important common denominator is that they strike us on a very deep emotional level, and the emotions are usually some of the deepest emotions that a human being can feel: heroism, fear, grief, joy," said Peter Howe, whose career has included stints as director of photography at *Life* magazine and picture editor at the *New York Times* (www.cnn.com/2013/09/01/us/the-flag-iconic-images).

Activity 1: Looking at Iconic Images

Here are some examples you can use with students. (There are many more posted on this web page from CNN: www.cnn.com/2013/09/01/us/the-flag-iconic-images.) As students experience each one, see if they believe the image meets some or all of the criteria defined by Peter Howe.

"Migrant Mother" (Figure 10.2), a photo taken in 1936 by Farm Security Administration photographer Dorothea Lange, might be described as iconic. The image of a 32-year-old mother of seven children during the Great Depression still appears today in the news when graphic designers are seeking an image to accompany a story about economic hard times.

"Flag Raising at Iwo Jima" (Figure 10.3) was taken by news photographer Joe Rosenthal, and its publication in newspapers during WWII became a symbol of American victory in the Pacific.

Figure 10.2 "Migrant Mother" by Dorothea Lange

Figure 10.3 "Flag Raising at Iwo Jima" by Joe Rosenthal

Figure 10.4 Lee Harvey Oswald as he was shot by Jack Ruby

Lee Harvey Oswald was shot and killed by Jack Ruby and that moment was captured by a photographer in Dallas, Texas, in the days following the assassination of President Kennedy (Figure 10.4).

Activity 2: Now You Find the Image

Can your students come up with other, more recent examples? Perhaps from 9–11, the Gulf Oil Spill, the wars in Iraq and Afghanistan, or closer to home? Although they may not remember some images personally, web searches will reveal many curated collections.

Another interesting question students might explore is this: How likely is it that a recent, popular social media image will stand the test of time and become truly "iconic"? (There's no shortage of examples to consider: www.hlntv.com/slideshow/2014/12/08/2014s-best-viral-photos-year.)

Powerful images, especially those in the news, offer educators another visual literacy "teachable moment" opportunity. These photos are easily accessible because they're part of our news feeds, our morning newspapers, the weekly news magazines, and social media messages. Using these images in instruction also helps meet the Common Core (English language arts) standards for "close reading," "visual literacy," and "informational texts."

Activity 3: Zoom in on a Photo

I like to start with a video I recently discovered. "Explain the Image," produced by the Critical Thinking Consortium, is an excellent introduction for students to how to "read" a photograph. In the video, available online (http://tc2.ca/explainTheImage.html), the host uses a worksheet to help guide students in their interpretation and analysis. You can download the worksheet here (see page 8 of the pdf document): http://tc2.ca/uploads/PDFs/T4T%20Samples/Explain_the_image_Tutorial.pdf.

Next, I like to present students with a photo without its caption. It could be an image from current news, history, or popular culture. Of course, students will have no context and in many cases, no prior knowledge. That's OK. Imagine students are looking at a picture of the Hindenburg disaster. With no caption to read, they are forced to look only at the photo, and to make judgments and inferences.

I like to start with the simple question: "What do you see?" Projecting the image on a SmartBoard or video screen is always helpful, because seeing it projected larger helps reveal details.

This process also helps introduce students to some of the rules of photography. If they're not already familiar with depth-of-field or the rule of thirds (among many others), now would be a good time to introduce these. (An excellent resource is the International Center of Photography's curriculum: www.icp.org/school/teacher-family-resources.) Your visual arts teacher is another resource for helping you and your students better understand this kind of visual literacy.

We've all heard the expression "a picture is worth a thousand words." I believe that photography is closely connected with literacy. Show someone a photo of your family or a picture from a vacation, and invariably you'll be describing in detail the people or the event or something else meaningful. Telling the story of a picture may spark a thousand words, in fact.

Every one of the iconic images I've shared in this chapter has a story behind it. Your students could investigate the story behind the image. Students can research the photographer and the circumstances surrounding how the image came to become iconic. I also encourage you to think about how you might use memorable images as jumping-off points to stimulate your students' writing in both non-fiction and fiction.

Our students are now constant consumers of visual information. These skills are vital to their critical thinking, problem-solving, and effective citizenship.

Additional Resources

I highly recommend the Capturing History series (www.capstonepub.com/library/products/captured-history-1) published by Capstone Press. Each book in the series focuses on one iconic image in history (e.g., first man on the moon) and the story behind it.

Another weekly resource is "What's Going on in This Picture"? (http://learning.blogs.nytimes.com/category/lesson-plans/whats-going-on-in-this-picture/?_r=0–), a free service that's part of the *New York Times* Learning Network.

Finally, I found the blog Reading the Pictures (www.readingthepictures.org) to be one of the best online. The site is "dedicated to visual politics, media literacy and the analysis of news images."

LESSON 28

The Role of Celebrity in Raising Our Awareness

Background

Powerful images have a way of making us remember important people and events. And photographs, seen by millions of people, also have a way of raising consciousness about issues, many of them tied to health and gender awareness. When a cultural icon becomes associated with deadly illness or controversial lifestyle, perception shifts. Students need to be aware of this important aspect of media literacy.

Consider these examples:

July 4, 1939: For many baseball fans, this date is etched in their memories. On that day New York Yankee Lou Gehrig retired, making the announcement before 69,000+ fans, saying he considered himself to be "the luckiest man on the face of the Earth." According to reports there was not a dry eye among the thousands of fans who watched at Yankee Stadium. The reason for his retirement: doctors had diagnosed him with a rare form of amyotrophic lateral sclerosis (ALS) disease, a condition which would from then on be known as "Lou Gehrig's Disease." His retirement also meant the end of a record 2,130 consecutive games-playing streak. He put a face on the disease.

Forty-six years later, on July 25, 1985: Actor Rock Hudson, a matinee idol to millions of women, issued a press release to say he had AIDS (Acquired Immune Deficiency Syndrome). The handsome, virile film star had appeared gaunt in public and there was much speculation about his declining health. "His illness and death have moved the fight against AIDS ahead more in three months than anything in the past three years," said Bruce Decker, chairman of California's AIDS Advisory Board Committee. Rock Hudson put a face on the disease.

Six years later, on November 7, 1991: Basketball mega-star Earvin "Magic" Johnson retired from the NBA because he was HIV-positive. CNN, the only all-news cable network at the time, carried the announcement live. He has helped educate millions about the disease. Like Rock Hudson, Magic also helped put a face on the virus related to AIDS.

November 1998: Actor Michael J. Fox revealed that seven years earlier he had been diagnosed with Parkinson's disease, "a progressive degeneration that ultimately renders some patients unable to walk, talk or take care of themselves" (www.cnn.com/SHOWBIZ/TV/9811/25/fox.parkinsons). He had just undergone a surgical procedure to lessen the disease's effects.

Despite his prognosis, Fox has continued to perform on television and lead the fight to find a cure. Fox helped put a face on the disease and inspire others with Parkinson's.

May 14, 2013: Actress Angelina Jolie published an op-ed in the *New York Times* explaining why she decided to undergo preventive double mastectomy. Because of an extensive family history of breast and ovarian cancer and having the BRCA1 gene mutation that dramatically raised her risk of cancer, she made the decision she called "my medical choice." Her surgery and decision helped raise awareness about genetic markers and preventive action (www.nytimes.com/2013/05/14/opinion/my-medical-choice.html?smid=tw-share&_r=1).

April/May 2015: *Vanity Fair* magazine and ABC-TV helped former Olympic gold medalist Bruce Jenner reveal to the world that he is now a woman who prefers to be called Caitlyn. An interview the 65-year-old Jenner gave to ABC's Diane Sawyer was watched by almost 17 million people (http://variety.com/2015/tv/news/bruce-jenner-interview-ratings-17-million-watch-abc-special-1201479968). Pop culture photographer Annie Leibowitz got the *Vanity Fair* cover assignment revealing the new look. Gossip tabloids and websites had been publishing mostly unflattering photos of Jenner for more than year, speculating on his conversion. As transgender people seek recognition and acceptance, Jenner's visual "reveal" helped put a face on this issue.

Activity: Looking at High-Impact Images and Stories

All these images and announcements helped tell important stories within the global arena of popular culture. Whether the storyteller is a celebrity or a new social media phenomenon, once they gain the stage, they can help explain their issue, disease, or condition to a world audience. They become tomorrow's water-cooler discussion topics, prompting debate and reflection, and even social action.

Have students consider the above celebrity scenarios and consider how the media became important agents not only by communicating (and sometimes sensationalizing) the news, but also by explaining it and educating news consumers. Ask students to discuss this question: Would the focus on health and gender issues have been as intense and long-lasting without the celebrity spokespersons?

Additional Resources

See "Close Reading of Media Texts," http://frankwbaker.com/mlc/close-reading-of-media-texts

Conclusion

Media literacy has been my passion for the past two decades. I have always been interested in helping new and seasoned educators understand its place in the curriculum. To spread the gospel of media literacy, I decided to go where the teachers reside: I realized that taking the message to teachers gathered at curriculum conferences, or district professional development days, was an early goal. These workshops are designed not only to introduce media literacy but also to demonstrate ways to engage students.

And how do we engage 21st-century learners? We don't have to go far.

A photo from the morning's news; a song from the latest playlist; the new sitcom on TV; the latest film release from Hollywood; a magazine or commercial – these are the media at your fingertips. The moment you demonstrate that you appreciate your students' media, and incorporate it in your instruction, you will have them hooked.

At the same time, I know that young people's fascination with the media makes "media literacy" not only important, but also necessary. Educators and parents must support the teaching of media analysis and media creation. Both are equally important. Schools that only invest and teach media production are only half fulfilling the media education promise.

Writing this book was a labor of love. Nothing pleased me more than to have this book endorsed both by MiddleWeb.com as well as the folks at Routledge. The ideas, resources, and activities contained herein are designed to make teaching media literacy easy for you to incorporate. I hope you find them to be that way.

I plan to continue submitting regular columns to MiddleWeb.com on these and other topics in the future, so I recommend you go there regularly.

In the meantime, I would enjoy hearing from you about what you think of this book and whether you tried these activities with your students. You can reach me via email: fbaker1346@gmail.com or via Twitter: @fbaker or through my Facebook page: www.facebook.com/Media-Literacy-Clearinghouse.

Glossary

ad, ads, advertisements: any paid message (print or non-print) produced by a sponsor, usually designed to inform, persuade, or sell

argument (as used in Common Core English language arts standards): "a reasoned, logical way of demonstrating that the writer's position, belief, or conclusion is valid. In English, students make claims about the worth or meaning of a literary work, defending their interpretation with evidence from the text, for example" (http://rpdp.net/files/ccss/ELA/ELA_11-12_Curr_Res/Writing%2011-12/Argument/Intro%20to%20Argument.pdf)

bias: "prejudice of, in favor or against one thing, person, or group compared with another, usually in a way considered unfair" (Oxford Dictionaries)

Black Friday: the day after Thanksgiving when many retailers have huge sales designed to pull in customers who are looking for bargains

Bloom's Digital Taxonomy: a revision to the traditional Bloom's taxonomy of higher-order thinking skills

buzz: used in viral marketing to describe efforts in advertising and marketing which result in customer interest

Children's Advertising Review Unit (CARU): a unit of the Better Business Bureau (BBB) responsible for analyzing children's advertising to insure it meets legal requirements and guidelines

close reading: a process whereby the reader goes deep into a reading to ask questions about the content, the author, and more

commercials: advertisements in video form

Common Core (teaching standards): a United States effort to create teaching guidelines in various subjects so that they are taught at approximately the same time, in those states that have adopted them

costume design: the process of identifying and creating clothes worn by actors in a stage, TV, or film production

creating/creation: "to bring something into existence" (Oxford Dictionaries)

critical inquiry: simply, asking questions

critical viewing skills: the application of critical thinking skills to visual media (images, moving images)

dark money: funds used in politics whose source is unknown

deconstruction: to take something apart to study it more closely

depth-of-field: "the distance between the nearest and furthest objects that give an image judged to be in focus in a camera" (Oxford Dictionaries)

diversity: "the state of being diverse; variety" (Oxford Dictionaries)
docudrama: a genre that blends elements of both documentary and drama
fact-check: the process by which news organizations investigate the accuracy of what is said by a candidate in speeches or in advertising
film literacy: understanding of how films communicate using the language of film
iconic: "of, relating to, or of the nature of an icon" (Oxford Dictionaries)
image: "A visible impression obtained by a camera, telescope, microscope, or other device, or displayed on a computer or video screen" (Oxford Dictionaries)
infographics: the visual representation of information
informational text: "text designed to convey factual information, rather than tell or advance a narrative. It may employ techniques such as lists, comparing and contrasting, or demonstrating cause and effect, and may be accompanied by graphs or charts" (www.chacha.com/question/what-is-a-definition-of-informational-text)
language of film: any number of tools or techniques used by creators to create or imply meaning
media: plural of medium
media literacy: the ability to access, analyze, evaluate, and produce communication in all forms
medium: a method of communication (radio, TV, film, newspapers, magazines, advertising, Internet, music) usually to large groups rather than face-to-face communication
National Council for the Social Studies (NCSS): umbrella organization which represents social studies educators in the U.S.
National Council of Teachers of English (NCTE): umbrella organization which represents teachers of English language arts in the U.S.
native advertising: "material in an online publication which resembles the publication's editorial content but is paid for by an advertiser and intended to promote the advertiser's product" (Oxford Dictionaries)
news literacy: "learn(ing) to judge the reliability of news reports and other sources of information that is passed along their social networks" (www.centerfornewsliteracy.org/what-is-news-literacy)
parody: "an imitation of the style of a particular writer, artist, or genre with deliberate exaggeration for comic effect" (Oxford Dictionaries)
persuasive technique (see propaganda techniques)
photojournalist: a journalist who is responsible not only for taking photographs for a news organization, but also for providing written descriptions for the images

PhotoShop: popular software used to enhance or alter an image
point-of-view (POV): perspective
polioptics: "influence-through-image: marries 'politics' with 'optics'" (www.polioptics.com/2010/09/polioptics-101)
production: the resulting product of a media work
product placement: the practice of paying for the placement of a product inside a medium
propaganda techniques: any one of a number of methods used to sway opinion or persuade an audience into thinking or believing something or someone
ratings (television): a number that estimates the size of the audience watching a particular program at a particular time, expressed as a percentage
remix: to mix again; to take unrelated media and edit them together
representation: the process by which a constructed media text stands for, symbolizes, describes, or represents people, places, events, or ideas that are real and have an existence outside the text (https://archive.groovy.net/jeffo/AMLoffline/content/med_glossary.html)
rule-of-thirds: in art and photography, a rule that breaks down an image into a tic-tac-toe division of nine separate elements
screenplay: a script written for television or film
skepticism: doubt about something seen, heard, or read
social media: "websites and applications that enable users to create and share content or to participate in social networking" (Oxford Dictionaries)
spot (see commercials)
upfront: an annual process whereby advertisers are presented with new TV programming and commit to fund the production prior to broadcast
visual literacy: the ability to read, deconstruct, and understand information presented visually